Breaking Free: A Practical Handbook for Escaping a Narcissist

Table of Contents

Welcome to "Breaking Free: A Practical Handbook for Escaping a Narcissist." This book is designed to be your guide, your companion, and your source of strength as you embark on one of the most challenging journeys of your life—leaving a narcissist. The path to freedom is rarely straightforward, often fraught with emotional turmoil, fear, and uncertainty. Yet, with every step you take, you move closer to reclaiming your life, your peace, and your happiness. The purpose of this book is to empower you with practical strategies, insightful advice, and the encouragement you need to break free from the grip of narcissistic abuse.

The decision to leave a narcissist is monumental. It signifies the beginning of a transformative journey, one that requires immense courage and resilience. This book acknowledges the difficulty of this decision and seeks to support you at every turn. Here, you will find a comprehensive guide to understanding narcissistic behavior, recognizing the signs of abuse, and taking the necessary steps to ensure your safety and well-being. You are not alone in this process. Many have walked this path before you and have found their way to a brighter, healthier future. Their stories, along with the expertise shared in this book, will serve as a beacon of hope and a testament to the possibility of change.

Taking the first step towards freedom is often the hardest. It means confronting uncomfortable truths, acknowledging the pain inflicted upon you, and accepting the necessity of change. This book aims to make that first step, and every subsequent step, a little less daunting.

By providing you with clear, actionable advice, it seeks to replace fear with knowledge and uncertainty with clarity. The journey may be long, and it may be difficult, but with each chapter, you will gain the tools and insights needed to navigate it successfully.

Understanding narcissism is crucial to breaking free from its grasp. Narcissists are often charming, persuasive, and manipulative, making it challenging to recognize their toxic influence. They can erode your self-esteem, isolate you from your support system, and make you doubt your reality. This book begins by shedding light on the characteristics of narcissistic personality disorder, helping you identify these traits in your partner. By understanding the nature of narcissism, you will be better equipped to see through the manipulations and understand the dynamics of your relationship.

Recognizing the signs of narcissistic abuse is a critical step in your journey. Many victims struggle with feelings of confusion and self-blame, often questioning whether the abuse is real or if they are overreacting. This book provides a detailed account of the red flags and warning signs associated with narcissistic behavior, helping you validate your experiences and understand that you are not to blame. By recognizing these signs, you can begin to dismantle the illusion created by the narcissist and see the truth of your situation.

Preparing to leave a narcissist involves careful planning and consideration. It is not a decision to be taken lightly, as narcissists can become volatile and aggressive when their control is threatened.

This book offers practical advice on creating a safety plan, gathering important documents, and building a support system. It emphasizes the importance of having a clear, strategic approach to leaving, ensuring that you are prepared for any potential obstacles. By taking these preparatory steps, you will be safeguarding your physical and emotional well-being, setting the stage for a successful escape.

The grey rock method, no contact rule, and other practical tactics for disengagement are essential tools in your arsenal. These strategies are designed to minimize the narcissist's power over you, helping you maintain your composure and protect your mental health. This book provides detailed instructions on how to implement these tactics effectively, using real-life examples and scenarios to illustrate their application. By mastering these techniques, you will be able to navigate interactions with the narcissist with greater confidence and control.

Leaving a narcissist often involves legal and financial considerations, especially if you share assets or have children together. This book addresses these critical aspects, offering guidance on understanding your rights, protecting your assets, and navigating custody arrangements. It stresses the importance of seeking legal advice and representation, ensuring that you are fully informed and supported throughout the process. By addressing these practical concerns, the book aims to provide a comprehensive approach to leaving, covering all facets of your situation.

Healing and moving forward is the ultimate goal of this journey.

Breaking free from a narcissist is not just about leaving; it is about rebuilding your life and reclaiming your sense of self. This book dedicates a significant portion to the healing process, offering strategies for rebuilding self-esteem, finding the right therapist, and creating a new life. It encourages you to set goals, rediscover your passions, and maintain your independence, fostering a sense of empowerment and resilience.

The conclusion of this book reinforces the importance of self-care and self-respect. It provides final encouragement, reminding you of the strength you possess and the progress you have made. It also offers a list of resources and further reading, ensuring that you have access to continued support and information. This final section serves as a reminder that while the journey may be challenging, it is also deeply rewarding, leading you to a life of freedom and fulfillment.

"Breaking Free: A Practical Handbook for Escaping a Narcissist" is more than just a book; it is a lifeline. It is a testament to the power of resilience and the possibility of change. As you turn each page, you will find practical advice, emotional support, and a clear path forward. Remember, you are not alone in this journey. Many have faced the same challenges and have emerged stronger and happier. With determination and the right guidance, you too can break free and reclaim your life.

Narcissistic Personality Disorder (NPD) is a mental condition characterized by an inflated sense of self-importance, an intense need for excessive attention and admiration, deeply troubled relationships, and a stark lack of empathy for others. This disorder falls under the category of personality disorders, which are enduring patterns of behavior, cognition, and inner experience that deviate markedly from the expectations of the individual's culture. These patterns are pervasive, inflexible, stable over time, and lead to distress or impairment. NPD is particularly complex, as it encompasses both grandiose and vulnerable aspects of narcissism, making it challenging to identify and understand fully.

Individuals with NPD exhibit grandiosity, where they possess an exaggerated sense of their own abilities and achievements. This grandiosity often manifests as a belief in their superiority over others, accompanied by an expectation to be recognized as superior without commensurate achievements. They may fantasize about unlimited success, power, brilliance, beauty, or ideal love. These fantasies are not just idle daydreams; they serve as a means for the individual to maintain their self-esteem and sense of worth. When these fantasies are challenged by reality, individuals with NPD may experience significant distress and may react with rage or defiance.

A hallmark of narcissistic behavior is a sense of entitlement. This means that individuals with NPD believe they deserve special treatment and adherence to their expectations by others. They may expect others to cater to their needs without question and become impatient or angry when this does not happen.

This sense of entitlement often leads to exploitative behavior. Narcissists tend to use others to achieve their own ends, showing little regard for the feelings or needs of those they exploit. This exploitative behavior can strain relationships, as others may feel used or manipulated.

Interpersonal relationships are particularly challenging for individuals with NPD. They often display a lack of genuine empathy, making it difficult for them to understand or share the feelings of others. This lack of empathy can lead to a dismissive or contemptuous attitude toward others, especially when others' needs or emotions do not align with their own. Narcissists may dominate conversations, steering the focus back to themselves and their achievements while minimizing or ignoring the contributions of others. They may also react negatively to criticism or perceived slights, often with anger or defensiveness, as their fragile self-esteem cannot tolerate any threat to their grandiose self-image.

Despite their outward confidence, individuals with NPD are often highly sensitive to any form of criticism or rejection. This vulnerability is a critical aspect of NPD, as it underpins much of their behavior. When faced with failure or criticism, they may react with narcissistic rage, a disproportionate and often aggressive response intended to protect their self-image. This rage can be verbal or physical and is typically aimed at whoever they perceive as the source of their discomfort. Alternatively, they may become sullen, withdrawn, or depressed, internalizing the criticism in a way that exacerbates their feelings of inadequacy and unworthiness.

In addition to these traits, individuals with NPD may exhibit arrogant or haughty behaviors. They may belittle or demean those they perceive as inferior, often to bolster their own sense of superiority. This condescending attitude can be particularly damaging in professional or personal relationships, where mutual respect and cooperation are essential. Their need to be the center of attention can also lead to attention-seeking behaviors, where they go to great lengths to ensure they remain in the spotlight, sometimes resorting to deceit or manipulation.

Identifying a narcissist involves observing a consistent pattern of these behaviors over time. One key indicator is their interpersonal style, which is often characterized by a lack of genuine interest in others unless it serves their own needs. They may initially appear charming and charismatic, using flattery and manipulation to win people over. However, this charm is usually superficial, as their primary interest lies in gaining admiration and control rather than forming authentic connections. Over time, the lack of depth in their relationships becomes apparent as they repeatedly fail to reciprocate emotional intimacy or show concern for others' welfare.

Another crucial aspect of identifying narcissists is their reaction to feedback. While everyone has a natural aversion to criticism, individuals with NPD display an extreme and often disproportionate response. They may respond with anger, denial, or attempts to discredit the source of the feedback, demonstrating an inability to process and learn from criticism constructively. This defensive behavior serves to protect their fragile self-esteem, which is constantly at risk of being shattered by any suggestion of imperfection.

Narcissists often have an inflated sense of their own abilities and achievements, which may lead them to overestimate their competence in various areas. This overestimation can result in risky or unethical behavior, as they may take on tasks or make decisions beyond their actual capabilities, driven by their need to maintain their grandiose self-image. When reality fails to meet their inflated expectations, they may blame others or external circumstances rather than acknowledging their own limitations.

In terms of social dynamics, narcissists often seek out positions of power and authority where their need for admiration can be more easily fulfilled. They may thrive in environments that reward self-promotion and competitiveness, but their inability to collaborate and empathize with others can ultimately undermine their success. Their leadership style may be autocratic and dismissive of others' contributions, leading to high turnover rates and a toxic work environment.

It is important to note that not all individuals with narcissistic traits meet the criteria for NPD. The diagnosis of NPD is reserved for those whose narcissistic traits cause significant impairment or distress in their lives. This diagnosis should be made by a qualified mental health professional who can assess the individual's history, behavior patterns, and the impact of their traits on their functioning.

Understanding NPD is crucial for those who may be in close contact with individuals exhibiting these traits, whether in personal or professional settings.

It can help in setting boundaries and managing interactions in a way that minimizes potential harm. For those with NPD, seeking professional help can be a significant step towards managing their symptoms and improving their relationships. Therapy, particularly cognitive-behavioral approaches, can help individuals with NPD develop greater self-awareness, empathy, and healthier ways of relating to others.

Narcissistic Personality Disorder is a complex and multifaceted condition that affects both the individual and those around them. It is characterized by grandiosity, a need for admiration, a sense of entitlement, exploitative behaviors, and a lack of empathy. Identifying a narcissist involves recognizing these patterns and understanding the underlying vulnerabilities that drive their behavior. While challenging to manage, awareness and professional intervention can lead to better outcomes for those affected by this disorder.

Identifying a narcissist involves a keen observation of consistent patterns in their behavior, attitudes, and interactions with others. Narcissists exhibit a range of traits and behaviors that can be both overt and subtle, making it important to understand these signs in various contexts. The identification process is not straightforward and often requires time and careful attention, as narcissists can initially present themselves in a charming and engaging manner, masking their true nature.

One of the most prominent signs of narcissism is an exaggerated sense of self-importance. Narcissists believe they are unique and superior to others, deserving of special treatment and recognition. This belief often translates into an overestimation of their abilities and achievements, coupled with an expectation that others should acknowledge their perceived superiority. They may frequently talk about their successes, often embellishing or fabricating stories to enhance their image. This self-centered narrative can dominate conversations, leaving little room for others to share their experiences or viewpoints.

A key characteristic of narcissists is their need for excessive admiration and validation. They constantly seek out praise and affirmation from those around them, often manipulating situations to ensure they remain the focus of attention. This need for admiration can manifest in various ways, such as fishing for compliments, boasting about their accomplishments, or becoming upset when they feel they are not receiving the recognition they deserve. Their self-esteem is fragile, and they rely heavily on external validation to maintain their self-image. When admiration is not forthcoming, they may react with anger, frustration, or even depressive symptoms, revealing their underlying insecurities.

Entitlement is another significant trait of narcissists. They believe they deserve special treatment and that rules do not apply to them in the same way they do to others. This sense of entitlement can lead to exploitative behaviors, where they use others to achieve their own ends without regard for the consequences.

For instance, a narcissist may take credit for someone else's work, manipulate colleagues or friends to get what they want, or expect unwavering loyalty and support without reciprocating. Their relationships often feel one-sided, with the narcissist benefiting at the expense of others.

Narcissists also display a marked lack of empathy, which is the ability to understand and share the feelings of others. This lack of empathy can make them appear cold, insensitive, or indifferent to the needs and emotions of those around them. They may dismiss others' feelings, fail to recognize or acknowledge their pain, or react with contempt when others express vulnerability. This emotional disconnect is often most apparent in close relationships, where the narcissist's inability to empathize can cause significant distress and frustration for their partners, family members, or friends.

Grandiosity is another defining feature of narcissism. This can be seen in their grandiose fantasies about their future, where they envision themselves achieving unparalleled success, power, or fame. These fantasies are not grounded in reality and often serve as a defense mechanism to protect their fragile self-esteem. When their grandiose self-image is challenged by reality, they may react with anger, denial, or attempts to discredit the source of the challenge. Their inability to accept their own limitations or failures can lead to a cycle of unrealistic goal-setting and subsequent disappointment.

Narcissists often have a heightened sensitivity to criticism, which can trigger intense emotional reactions.

They may respond to any form of critique, no matter how constructive or mild, with defensiveness, anger, or attempts to undermine the credibility of the person offering the feedback. This hypersensitivity stems from their deep-seated insecurities and the constant need to protect their inflated self-image. In some cases, they may even engage in narcissistic rage, a disproportionate and aggressive response intended to intimidate or silence their critics. This reaction can be particularly pronounced in situations where their authority or competence is questioned.

Another aspect to consider when identifying a narcissist is their interpersonal style, which often involves manipulative and controlling behaviors. Narcissists may use charm and charisma to win people over initially, creating an impression of confidence and capability. However, this charm is typically superficial, and as relationships progress, the narcissist's true nature becomes apparent. They may use tactics such as gaslighting, where they manipulate others into doubting their own perceptions or memories, to maintain control and dominance. This manipulative behavior can create a toxic environment, where the narcissist's needs and desires consistently take precedence over those of others.

Narcissists also tend to be envious of others and believe that others are envious of them. This envy can drive them to undermine or sabotage those they perceive as threats to their own status or success. They may spread rumors, engage in backstabbing, or attempt to discredit others to elevate themselves.

This competitive and adversarial approach to relationships can create a hostile and divisive atmosphere, particularly in professional settings where collaboration and teamwork are essential.

In social situations, narcissists often seek out positions of power and authority, where their need for admiration and control can be more easily fulfilled. They may thrive in environments that reward self-promotion and assertiveness, but their inability to collaborate effectively or empathize with others can ultimately undermine their success. Their leadership style may be autocratic and dismissive of others' contributions, leading to high turnover rates and a toxic work culture. Over time, their lack of genuine concern for others and their self-serving behaviors can erode trust and cooperation within teams and organizations.

Recognizing these patterns requires a careful and sustained observation of the individual's behavior across different contexts. It is important to consider the consistency of these traits and behaviors, as everyone may exhibit narcissistic tendencies from time to time. However, for a diagnosis of Narcissistic Personality Disorder, these traits must be pervasive, inflexible, and lead to significant distress or impairment in the individual's life. A qualified mental health professional can provide a comprehensive assessment to determine whether someone meets the criteria for NPD.

Understanding the signs of narcissism is crucial for those who may be in close contact with individuals exhibiting these traits. It can help in setting boundaries and managing interactions in a way that minimizes potential harm.

For those dealing with narcissists, it is important to protect one's own mental and emotional well-being, as narcissists can be highly draining and manipulative. Seeking support from friends, family, or a mental health professional can be beneficial in navigating these challenging relationships.

Identifying a narcissist involves recognizing a consistent pattern of behaviors and traits, including an exaggerated sense of self-importance, a need for excessive admiration, entitlement, lack of empathy, grandiosity, sensitivity to criticism, manipulative behaviors, and envy. While these characteristics can be difficult to discern initially, especially given the narcissist's ability to present themselves in a favorable light, careful observation over time can reveal their true nature. Understanding these signs can help individuals protect themselves and make informed decisions about their relationships with narcissists.

Narcissistic abuse, a form of emotional and psychological maltreatment inflicted by individuals with Narcissistic Personality Disorder (NPD) or significant narcissistic traits, has profound and often devastating effects on its victims. The impact of this abuse can permeate various aspects of the victim's life, affecting their emotional, psychological, and even physical well-being. Understanding the far-reaching consequences of narcissistic abuse is crucial for recognizing the signs, seeking appropriate help, and fostering recovery.

Emotionally, victims of narcissistic abuse often experience a profound sense of confusion and self-doubt. Narcissists are adept at manipulating their victims through tactics like gaslighting, where they make the victim question their own reality, perceptions, and memories. This manipulation can lead to a pervasive sense of confusion and instability, as victims are constantly second-guessing their experiences and feelings. Over time, this can erode their self-confidence and self-esteem, leaving them feeling inadequate and unworthy. The relentless criticism and devaluation that characterize narcissistic abuse contribute to this emotional turmoil, as victims internalize the negative messages about themselves and their worth.

Psychologically, the effects of narcissistic abuse can be deeply damaging. Victims often develop symptoms of anxiety and depression, stemming from the chronic stress and emotional distress inflicted by the abuser. The unpredictable and often hostile behavior of the narcissist creates an environment of fear and hyper-vigilance, where the victim is constantly on edge, anticipating the next bout of anger or manipulation. This chronic stress can lead to anxiety disorders, characterized by persistent worry, nervousness, and an inability to relax. Depression is also common, as the constant emotional abuse and lack of support erode the victim's sense of hope and joy. Feelings of helplessness and despair become overwhelming, making it difficult for the victim to see a way out of their situation.

In addition to anxiety and depression, victims of narcissistic abuse may develop post-traumatic stress disorder (PTSD) or complex PTSD (C-PTSD).

The trauma of living with a narcissistic abuser, who can be emotionally volatile and manipulative, creates lasting psychological scars. Symptoms of PTSD and C-PTSD can include intrusive thoughts and memories, flashbacks, nightmares, and a heightened startle response. Victims may also experience emotional numbing, where they feel disconnected from their emotions and surroundings as a coping mechanism to deal with the overwhelming stress. These symptoms can severely impair the victim's ability to function in daily life, affecting their work, relationships, and overall well-being.

The impact of narcissistic abuse extends to the victim's social and relational spheres as well. Narcissists often isolate their victims from friends and family, creating a dependency on the abuser and cutting off external sources of support and validation. This isolation exacerbates the victim's sense of loneliness and helplessness, making it even harder for them to break free from the abusive relationship. The abuser's manipulation and control tactics can also damage the victim's other relationships, as they may become distrustful or withdrawn, fearing further betrayal or manipulation. This erosion of social support networks further deepens the victim's isolation and emotional distress.

Physically, the stress and trauma of narcissistic abuse can take a significant toll on the victim's health. Chronic stress can lead to a range of physical health issues, including headaches, gastrointestinal problems, and a weakened immune system. Victims may experience sleep disturbances, such as insomnia or nightmares, which further exacerbate their emotional and physical exhaustion.

Over time, the cumulative effects of chronic stress can contribute to more serious health conditions, such as cardiovascular disease and autoimmune disorders. The link between emotional trauma and physical health is well-documented, highlighting the need for comprehensive care that addresses both the psychological and physical aspects of recovery from narcissistic abuse.

The economic impact of narcissistic abuse should not be overlooked either. Narcissists may exert control over the victim's finances, restricting their access to money and resources as a means of maintaining power and dependency. This financial abuse can leave victims financially destitute and unable to escape the abusive relationship due to a lack of resources. Even after leaving the abuser, victims may struggle with financial instability, as the long-term effects of the abuse hinder their ability to rebuild their lives and regain financial independence.

Recovering from narcissistic abuse is a challenging and multifaceted process. Victims often need to rebuild their self-esteem and sense of self-worth, which have been systematically eroded by the abuser. Therapy, particularly trauma-informed approaches, can be instrumental in helping victims process their experiences, heal from trauma, and develop healthier coping mechanisms. Support groups and networks can provide essential emotional support and validation, helping victims feel less isolated and more understood. Establishing boundaries and learning to trust again are crucial steps in the recovery process, enabling victims to protect themselves from future abuse and rebuild their lives.

The impact of narcissistic abuse on victims is profound and multifaceted, affecting their emotional, psychological, physical, social, and economic well-being. The manipulation, devaluation, and control exerted by narcissists leave lasting scars that can take years to heal. Recognizing the signs of narcissistic abuse and understanding its consequences are vital for victims to seek appropriate help and support. Recovery is possible, but it requires a comprehensive and compassionate approach that addresses the diverse and complex effects of this insidious form of abuse.

"When a toxic person can no longer control you, they will try to control how others see you. The misinformation will feel unfair, but you stay above it, trusting that other people will eventually see the truth just like you did." – Jill Blakeway

Chapter 1: Recognizing the Signs

Recognizing the signs of narcissistic behavior is essential for protecting oneself from potential harm. Narcissists employ a variety of behaviors and tactics to manipulate and control their victims, often leaving significant emotional and psychological damage in their wake. Understanding these red flags and warning signs can help individuals identify narcissists early on and take necessary steps to safeguard their well-being.

One of the most prominent behaviors exhibited by narcissists is an exaggerated sense of self-importance. Narcissists believe they are superior to others and expect to be treated as such. They often boast about their achievements and talents, regardless of whether their claims are based in reality. This grandiosity extends to their expectations of admiration and validation from others. Narcissists crave constant attention and praise and may go to great lengths to ensure they remain the center of attention. They may monopolize conversations, steer discussions back to themselves, and dismiss or belittle others' contributions. This relentless need for admiration and recognition is a key red flag of narcissistic behavior.

Entitlement is another significant characteristic of narcissists. They believe they deserve special treatment and that the rules do not apply to them in the same way they do to others. This sense of entitlement can manifest in various ways, such as expecting others to cater to their needs without reciprocating, taking advantage of others' generosity, and showing little regard for boundaries. Narcissists often view others as extensions of themselves, existing primarily to serve their needs and desires.

This exploitative behavior is a clear warning sign of narcissism, as it demonstrates a fundamental lack of empathy and respect for others.

Lack of empathy is a hallmark trait of narcissists. They have difficulty understanding or caring about the feelings and needs of others. This emotional disconnect allows them to manipulate and exploit people without remorse. Narcissists may feign empathy when it serves their interests, but their concern is typically shallow and self-serving. This lack of genuine empathy can lead to callous and insensitive behavior, as narcissists prioritize their own needs and desires above all else. In relationships, this often translates to a lack of emotional support and validation, leaving their partners feeling neglected and unimportant.

Manipulation is a common tactic used by narcissists to control and dominate others. They are skilled at identifying and exploiting the vulnerabilities of those around them. This can involve a range of behaviors, from subtle manipulation to outright deceit. Gaslighting, a particularly insidious form of manipulation, involves making the victim doubt their own perceptions and reality. Narcissists may deny things they have said or done, accuse the victim of being overly sensitive or paranoid, and create a distorted narrative that places them in a favorable light. This tactic can leave victims feeling confused, disoriented, and dependent on the narcissist for validation and reality-checking.

Another red flag is the narcissist's tendency to devalue and criticize others. While they may initially shower their targets with praise and admiration, this phase often gives way to a pattern of devaluation.

Once the narcissist has secured the victim's trust and admiration, they begin to undermine their self-esteem through constant criticism and belittlement. This devaluation serves to maintain the narcissist's sense of superiority and control. Victims may find themselves walking on eggshells, constantly striving to meet the narcissist's ever-changing standards and avoid their wrath. This cycle of idealization and devaluation is a common tactic used to manipulate and dominate others.

Narcissists also exhibit a heightened sensitivity to criticism, often reacting with anger or defiance when their self-image is challenged. This hypersensitivity is rooted in their fragile self-esteem, which is heavily dependent on external validation. When faced with criticism or perceived slights, narcissists may lash out aggressively, employing tactics such as verbal abuse, character assassination, and intimidation to silence their critics and protect their ego. This volatile reaction to criticism is a significant warning sign, as it reveals the underlying insecurity and instability of the narcissist's self-image.

Another common behavior of narcissists is their propensity for envy and jealousy. Despite their outward confidence, narcissists are often deeply insecure and envious of others' success, talents, and relationships. They may attempt to undermine or sabotage those they perceive as threats to their own status and superiority. This envy can drive them to spread rumors, engage in backstabbing, and create divisions among colleagues, friends, and family members. The narcissist's need to be the best and have the best can lead to a toxic and competitive environment, where others are seen as rivals rather than collaborators or supporters.

In personal relationships, narcissists often display controlling and possessive behavior. They may seek to isolate their partners from friends and family, creating a dependency that allows them to exert greater control. This isolation can be achieved through subtle manipulation, such as criticizing the victim's loved ones or creating conflicts that drive a wedge between the victim and their support network. By cutting off external sources of support and validation, the narcissist ensures that their partner becomes increasingly reliant on them, making it harder for the victim to recognize and escape the abusive dynamics.

Narcissists are also known for their tendency to shift blame and avoid accountability. They rarely take responsibility for their actions and are quick to deflect blame onto others. When confronted with their behavior, narcissists may employ tactics such as projection, accusing others of the very faults and misdeeds they themselves are guilty of. This deflection serves to protect their self-image and avoid the discomfort of introspection and accountability. Victims of narcissistic abuse often find themselves unfairly blamed for problems and conflicts, adding to their confusion and distress.

Grandiosity in narcissists often extends to their fantasies and aspirations. They may harbor unrealistic and grandiose dreams of unlimited success, power, beauty, or brilliance. These fantasies are a coping mechanism to bolster their fragile self-esteem and distract from their underlying insecurities. Narcissists may seek out positions of power and authority, where their need for admiration and control can be more easily fulfilled.

However, their inability to collaborate and empathize with others often undermines their long-term success, leading to conflicts and instability in their professional and personal lives.

The superficial charm of narcissists can be another red flag. Initially, they may present themselves as charismatic, confident, and engaging, using charm to win over their targets. This charm is often a facade, designed to manipulate and draw people into their orbit. As the relationship progresses, the narcissist's true nature becomes apparent, revealing a pattern of self-centeredness, manipulation, and abuse. The contrast between the initial charm and the subsequent abusive behavior can be jarring and disorienting for victims, making it difficult to reconcile the two and recognize the narcissist's true intentions.

In addition to these behaviors, narcissists often exhibit a lack of long-term, stable relationships. Their inability to empathize and constant need for validation make it difficult for them to maintain healthy, reciprocal relationships. Instead, they may have a history of short-term, tumultuous relationships characterized by intense highs and lows. The pattern of idealization and devaluation often leads to frequent breakups and conflicts, as partners eventually tire of the narcissist's manipulative and abusive behavior. This instability in relationships is a key indicator of narcissistic tendencies.

Recognizing these red flags and warning signs is crucial for identifying narcissists and protecting oneself from their harmful behavior.

While everyone may exhibit some narcissistic traits occasionally, it is the pervasive, consistent, and extreme nature of these behaviors that distinguishes pathological narcissism from normal self-centeredness. By understanding these signs, individuals can take proactive steps to safeguard their well-being, set healthy boundaries, and seek support when needed.

Awareness and education about narcissistic behavior are essential for fostering resilience and empowering individuals to recognize and respond to narcissistic abuse. Support networks, therapy, and self-care strategies can play a vital role in helping victims recover and rebuild their lives after experiencing narcissistic abuse. Recognizing the signs early on can prevent deeper emotional and psychological harm, enabling individuals to make informed decisions about their relationships and interactions with potential narcissists.

Narcissists employ a range of behaviors and tactics to manipulate and control their victims, including an exaggerated sense of self-importance, entitlement, lack of empathy, manipulation, devaluation, hypersensitivity to criticism, envy, controlling behavior, blame-shifting, grandiosity, superficial charm, and unstable relationships. Recognizing these red flags and warning signs is crucial for identifying narcissists and protecting oneself from their harmful impact. By understanding these behaviors, individuals can take steps to safeguard their well-being, set boundaries, and seek support, ultimately fostering resilience and recovery from narcissistic abuse.

The emotional and psychological effects of narcissistic abuse on victims are profound and far-reaching, often leaving deep and lasting scars. Narcissistic abuse, characterized by manipulation, devaluation, and emotional cruelty, systematically erodes the victim's sense of self and mental well-being. Understanding these effects is crucial for recognizing the signs of abuse and providing appropriate support and intervention.

Emotionally, victims of narcissistic abuse often experience intense feelings of confusion, self-doubt, and worthlessness. The narcissist's manipulative tactics, such as gaslighting, are designed to make the victim question their own perceptions and reality. Gaslighting involves denying events, distorting the truth, and shifting blame onto the victim, creating a sense of disorientation and mistrust in one's own memory and judgment. Over time, this manipulation can lead victims to doubt their sanity, making them increasingly dependent on the narcissist for validation and reality-checking. The constant second-guessing erodes their self-confidence and self-esteem, leading to feelings of inadequacy and unworthiness.

The cycle of idealization and devaluation, a hallmark of narcissistic relationships, further compounds the emotional turmoil. In the initial stages of the relationship, the narcissist may shower the victim with praise, attention, and affection, creating an intense bond and a sense of being valued and loved. However, this phase is often followed by a period of devaluation, where the narcissist becomes critical, dismissive, and emotionally distant.

The abrupt shift from idealization to devaluation leaves victims feeling confused and abandoned, as they struggle to understand what went wrong and why they are no longer valued. This emotional rollercoaster can result in feelings of anxiety, depression, and despair.

Psychologically, the effects of narcissistic abuse can be severe and debilitating. Victims often develop symptoms of anxiety and depression as a result of the chronic stress and emotional trauma inflicted by the narcissist. Anxiety may manifest as persistent worry, nervousness, and a heightened state of alertness, as victims are constantly on edge, anticipating the narcissist's next outburst or manipulative tactic. This chronic state of hyper-vigilance can lead to sleep disturbances, physical health issues, and a general sense of exhaustion and burnout.

Depression is also a common consequence of narcissistic abuse. The relentless criticism, emotional neglect, and devaluation leave victims feeling hopeless and despairing. They may experience a loss of interest in activities they once enjoyed, feelings of worthlessness and guilt, and a pervasive sense of sadness and emptiness. In severe cases, victims may have suicidal thoughts or tendencies, highlighting the critical need for support and intervention. The depression resulting from narcissistic abuse is often compounded by the victim's isolation, as the narcissist typically works to sever their connections with friends and family, leaving them without a support network.

Victims of narcissistic abuse may also develop post-traumatic stress disorder (PTSD) or complex PTSD (C-PTSD).

The trauma of living with a narcissistic abuser, characterized by unpredictable and often violent emotional outbursts, manipulation, and control, creates lasting psychological scars. Symptoms of PTSD and C-PTSD can include intrusive thoughts and memories, flashbacks, nightmares, and a heightened startle response. Victims may also experience emotional numbing, where they feel disconnected from their emotions and surroundings as a coping mechanism to deal with the overwhelming stress. These symptoms can severely impair the victim's ability to function in daily life, affecting their work, relationships, and overall well-being.

The impact of narcissistic abuse extends to the victim's self-identity and sense of self-worth. Narcissists systematically undermine their victims' confidence and self-esteem through constant criticism, belittlement, and devaluation. This ongoing assault on their sense of self-worth can lead to a profound identity crisis, where victims struggle to recognize their own value and abilities. They may internalize the negative messages from the narcissist, believing they are unworthy, inadequate, and incapable. This shattered self-esteem makes it difficult for victims to assert themselves, set boundaries, or pursue their goals and dreams, perpetuating a cycle of dependency and low self-worth.

The psychological effects of narcissistic abuse also include a pervasive sense of helplessness and powerlessness. Narcissists exert control over every aspect of their victims' lives, dictating their actions, thoughts, and emotions. This constant control and manipulation erode the victim's sense of autonomy and agency, leaving them feeling trapped and unable to escape the abusive relationship.

The feeling of powerlessness is exacerbated by the narcissist's ability to manipulate and distort reality, making it difficult for victims to see a way out or believe that they have the strength and resources to leave.

In addition to these emotional and psychological effects, victims of narcissistic abuse often suffer from social and relational difficulties. Narcissists work to isolate their victims from friends, family, and other sources of support, creating a dependency on the abuser. This isolation not only deepens the victim's sense of loneliness and despair but also makes it harder for them to seek help and support. Even after leaving the narcissistic relationship, victims may struggle to rebuild their social networks and trust others, as the trauma of the abuse leaves them wary of forming new relationships.

The long-term psychological impact of narcissistic abuse can also affect victims' future relationships. The trauma and emotional damage inflicted by the narcissist can lead to difficulties in trusting others, setting healthy boundaries, and maintaining healthy, reciprocal relationships. Victims may find themselves drawn to similar toxic relationships, repeating patterns of abuse and manipulation. This cycle can be broken through therapy and self-awareness, but it requires time, effort, and support to heal and develop healthier relational patterns.

The emotional and psychological effects of narcissistic abuse on victims are profound and far-reaching. The manipulation, devaluation, and emotional cruelty characteristic of narcissistic behavior systematically erode the victim's self-esteem, self-worth, and mental well-being.

Victims often experience intense feelings of confusion, self-doubt, anxiety, depression, and a sense of helplessness and powerlessness. The trauma of narcissistic abuse can lead to PTSD or C-PTSD, affecting the victim's ability to function in daily life and maintain healthy relationships. Recognizing these effects is crucial for providing appropriate support and intervention, helping victims heal and rebuild their lives after the devastating impact of narcissistic abuse.

Identifying whether you are in a relationship with a narcissist can be challenging, especially given the manipulative nature of narcissistic behavior. Narcissists often mask their true selves behind charm and manipulation, making it difficult to recognize the signs until significant emotional and psychological harm has occurred. The following self-assessment questions can help you determine if your relationship might be characterized by narcissistic abuse. Reflect honestly on your experiences and feelings as you consider these questions.

Emotional Manipulation and Control
1. Do you often feel confused about your partner's behavior and question your own perceptions?
   - Narcissists frequently engage in gaslighting, making you doubt your reality and feel uncertain about your experiences.

2. Does your partner frequently shift the blame onto you for problems or conflicts in the relationship?
   - Narcissists rarely take responsibility for their actions and often make you feel at fault for issues they cause.

3. Do you feel like you are walking on eggshells, constantly trying to avoid upsetting your partner?
   - The unpredictable nature of a narcissist's anger or displeasure can create a tense and fearful environment.

Lack of Empathy and Emotional Support
4. Does your partner show a lack of genuine interest or empathy towards your feelings and experiences?
 - A hallmark of narcissistic behavior is a profound lack of empathy, making it difficult for them to understand or care about your emotions.

5. Do you feel emotionally neglected or invalidated by your partner?
 - Narcissists often dismiss or belittle your feelings, leaving you feeling unsupported and insignificant.

6. Does your partner seem to prioritize their needs and desires above yours consistently?
 - Narcissists have an inflated sense of entitlement and expect their needs to come first, often at your expense.

Idealization and Devaluation
7. Did your relationship start with intense admiration and affection, only to shift to criticism and devaluation?
 - Narcissists typically begin relationships with excessive flattery and attention, followed by a phase of harsh criticism and emotional withdrawal.

8. Does your partner frequently criticize, belittle, or undermine you?
 - The devaluation phase involves constant criticism and negative comments aimed at diminishing your self-esteem.

9. Do you feel that your partner's love and affection are conditional and can be withdrawn at any moment?
 - Narcissists often use affection and approval as tools to control and manipulate, making you feel unworthy and insecure.

Control and Isolation
10. Does your partner try to control who you spend time with or isolate you from friends and family?
   - Narcissists often seek to isolate you from your support network to increase their control and dependency.

11. Do you feel like your partner monitors your activities and communications excessively?
   - Narcissists may exhibit controlling behavior by closely monitoring your interactions and whereabouts.

12. Has your partner ever discouraged or sabotaged your personal goals and ambitions?
   - Narcissists often feel threatened by your success and may undermine your efforts to maintain control over you.

Self-Esteem and Personal Growth
13. Do you feel that your self-esteem has significantly decreased since being in the relationship?
   - Constant criticism and manipulation can erode your self-confidence and sense of self-worth.

14. Do you feel dependent on your partner for validation and self-worth?
   - Narcissists create a dynamic where you seek their approval to feel valued, making you more reliant on them.

15. Have you noticed a decline in your mental or emotional well-being since the relationship began?
   - The stress and emotional turmoil of a narcissistic relationship can lead to anxiety, depression, and other mental health issues.

Gaslighting and Reality Distortion

16. Does your partner frequently deny things they have said or done, making you question your memory?
   - Gaslighting involves denying or twisting the truth to make you doubt your recollections and feel disoriented.

17. Do you feel that your partner's version of events often differs significantly from your own?
   - Narcissists create a distorted narrative that suits their needs, often making you doubt your own experiences.

18. Have you ever felt like you're losing your sense of self or identity in the relationship?
   - Narcissists manipulate and control to the extent that you may lose touch with your own needs, desires, and sense of self.

Seeking External Validation

19. Does your partner require constant admiration and validation from others?
   - Narcissists have an insatiable need for admiration and may seek it from multiple sources, often at the expense of your feelings.

20. Does your partner exhibit jealousy or envy towards others' achievements and successes?
   - Despite their outward confidence, narcissists are often deeply insecure and envious of others, leading to competitive or sabotaging behavior.

21. Do you feel that your partner is more concerned with maintaining their image than the health of the relationship?
   - Narcissists prioritize their public image and reputation over genuine connection and relationship health.

Reflecting on the Relationship

22. Do you feel more drained and exhausted than fulfilled in the relationship?
- Narcissistic relationships are emotionally taxing and often leave you feeling depleted rather than supported and fulfilled.

23. Do you find yourself making excuses for your partner's behavior to friends, family, or even yourself?
- Victims of narcissistic abuse often rationalize their partner's actions to make sense of the chaos and maintain a semblance of stability.

24. Have you tried to set boundaries with your partner, only to have them ignored or violated?
- Narcissists frequently disregard boundaries, viewing them as challenges to their control and manipulation.

If you find yourself answering "yes" to many of these questions, it may indicate that you are in a relationship with a narcissist. Recognizing these signs is the first step towards understanding your situation and seeking the necessary support and resources to address it. Narcissistic abuse can have profound emotional and psychological effects, and acknowledging the reality of your relationship is crucial for your well-being and recovery. Consider reaching out to a trusted friend, therapist, or support group to help you navigate this challenging experience and reclaim your sense of self and autonomy.

Understanding your own vulnerabilities and triggers is a crucial step in protecting yourself from narcissistic abuse and fostering emotional resilience. Vulnerabilities are aspects of your personality or past experiences that may make you more susceptible to manipulation and control. These can include low self-esteem, a history of trauma or abuse, a deep need for approval and validation, and difficulty setting and enforcing personal boundaries. Recognizing these vulnerabilities allows you to be more aware of how they might influence your interactions and relationships, particularly with narcissistic individuals who are adept at exploiting them. For example, if you have a strong desire to be liked and accepted, a narcissist may use flattery and attention to draw you in, only to later manipulate and control you through criticism and devaluation. Triggers, on the other hand, are specific stimuli or situations that provoke a strong emotional response, often tied to past traumas or unresolved issues. Identifying your triggers can help you anticipate and manage your reactions in situations where you might otherwise feel overwhelmed or distressed. For instance, if being ignored or dismissed is a trigger for you, understanding this can help you recognize when a narcissist is using this tactic to manipulate you, allowing you to respond more effectively and maintain your emotional equilibrium. By gaining insight into your vulnerabilities and triggers, you can develop strategies to protect yourself, such as strengthening your self-esteem, practicing assertiveness, and seeking support from trusted friends or professionals. This self-awareness not only empowers you to navigate relationships more safely but also contributes to your overall emotional well-being and personal growth.

"Relationships with narcissists are held in place by the hope of a 'someday better,' with little evidence to support it will ever arrive."– Dr. Ramani

Creating a safety plan is a crucial step for anyone preparing to leave a narcissistic relationship. Ensuring both physical and emotional safety requires careful planning and consideration, as the process of leaving can be fraught with risks, particularly when dealing with a narcissistic partner who may react unpredictably or violently to losing control. This comprehensive safety plan involves several key steps that help safeguard your well-being during this vulnerable transition.

Firstly, it is essential to recognize the importance of physical safety. Narcissists can become volatile and aggressive when they sense they are losing control, so it is vital to have a clear, actionable escape plan. Begin by identifying a safe place to go, such as a trusted friend's or family member's home, a shelter, or a location where your partner is unlikely to find you. Ensure that this place is secure and that you have access to it at any time. Memorize important phone numbers, including those of close friends, family members, and local domestic violence hotlines, so you can quickly reach out for help if necessary.

Next, pack an emergency bag with essential items that you can quickly grab when you decide to leave. This bag should include important documents such as identification, passports, birth certificates, financial records, and any legal papers related to your situation, such as restraining orders or custody agreements. Also, pack clothes, medications, keys, some cash, and any necessary personal items. Store this bag in a discreet and accessible location, or with someone you trust, to ensure you can leave swiftly and safely when the time comes.

Financial independence is another critical aspect of your safety plan. Narcissistic partners often exert control through financial means, making it difficult for victims to leave due to financial dependency. Start by setting aside money in a separate account that your partner does not know about, if possible. Gradually save small amounts to avoid arousing suspicion. Additionally, consider seeking financial advice or assistance from a professional who can help you navigate your financial situation and ensure you have the resources to support yourself once you leave.

Building a support network is also vital for both your physical and emotional safety. Inform trusted friends, family members, or coworkers about your situation and your plan to leave. Having a support system in place provides emotional backing and practical assistance, such as transportation, temporary housing, or help with legal matters. Additionally, reach out to local organizations and support groups that specialize in helping victims of domestic abuse. These groups can offer valuable resources, counseling, and advocacy to support you through the process of leaving and rebuilding your life.

Legal considerations play a significant role in your safety plan. If you fear for your safety, consider obtaining a restraining order against your partner. Consult with a lawyer or a legal advocate who specializes in domestic violence cases to understand your rights and the legal steps you can take to protect yourself. They can help you navigate the legal system, file for protective orders, and address any custody or divorce issues that may arise. Having legal protection can deter your partner from attempting to contact or harm you, providing an additional layer of security.

Emotional safety is equally important during this tumultuous time. The process of leaving a narcissistic relationship can be emotionally draining and overwhelming. It is crucial to take steps to protect your mental health and well-being. Engage in self-care practices that help you manage stress and maintain your emotional balance. This can include regular exercise, meditation, journaling, or any activity that brings you peace and relaxation. Consider seeking therapy or counseling to work through the emotional trauma and to develop coping strategies for dealing with the aftermath of the relationship. A professional therapist can provide a safe space to express your feelings, gain clarity, and build resilience.

Communication safety is another crucial element of your plan. Narcissistic partners often monitor their victim's communications to maintain control. Ensure that your digital devices are secure by changing passwords and using two-factor authentication. Be cautious about the information you share on social media and consider blocking your partner or adjusting your privacy settings to prevent them from accessing your posts. If necessary, use a different phone or email account for planning your escape and communicating with your support network. Keeping your communication private and secure can prevent your partner from intercepting your plans and retaliating.

It is also important to consider the logistics of leaving. Plan the best time to leave, ideally when your partner is not at home or is less likely to notice your absence immediately. This can give you a head start and reduce the risk of confrontation. If you have children, plan for their safety and well-being as well.

Ensure they understand the plan, if appropriate for their age, and make arrangements for their schooling and care. If possible, coordinate with your support network to assist with the logistics, such as transportation and temporary housing.

Finally, prepare for the aftermath of leaving. Narcissists often react with rage, vindictiveness, or attempts to hoover (lure you back into the relationship) when they realize they have lost control. Be mentally and emotionally prepared for these reactions and have a plan in place to handle them. This might include changing your phone number, securing your home, and being vigilant about your surroundings. Stay connected with your support network and continue seeking professional help to navigate the emotional and psychological challenges that may arise.

Creating a comprehensive safety plan involves multiple steps to ensure both physical and emotional safety when leaving a narcissistic relationship. Recognize the importance of securing a safe place, packing an emergency bag, achieving financial independence, building a support network, addressing legal considerations, protecting your emotional well-being, securing your communications, planning the logistics of leaving, and preparing for the aftermath. By taking these steps, you can protect yourself from potential harm, regain control over your life, and begin the journey towards healing and recovery. Remember, leaving a narcissistic relationship is a courageous and empowering step, and having a well-thought-out safety plan is essential for your safety and peace of mind.

Gathering important documents and financial resources is a critical step when preparing to leave a narcissistic relationship. Ensuring you have access to necessary paperwork and financial assets provides a foundation for independence and security. Start by collecting essential identification documents, such as passports, birth certificates, social security cards, and driver's licenses for yourself and any children involved. These documents are vital for accessing services, employment, and housing. Additionally, gather financial records, including bank statements, credit card bills, tax returns, and investment information. Having a clear understanding of your financial situation is crucial for planning your future. Secure these documents in a safe place, ideally outside the home, such as with a trusted friend or family member, or in a safety deposit box. In parallel, work towards establishing financial independence by opening a separate bank account in your name, if possible, and gradually saving money to ensure you have funds to support yourself during the transition. This might involve discreetly setting aside cash or using a secret account that your partner is unaware of. If you are employed, consider having your salary directly deposited into your new account. Access to financial resources can be a significant barrier to leaving, so explore options for financial assistance through local support organizations, legal aid, or government programs designed to help those escaping abusive relationships. By gathering important documents and securing financial resources, you equip yourself with the tools necessary to take decisive action, protect your well-being, and build a stable foundation for your future away from the narcissistic partner.

Building a robust support system is crucial when preparing to leave a narcissistic relationship. This network of trusted friends and family members plays a pivotal role in providing emotional support, practical assistance, and a sense of safety during what can be a tumultuous and challenging transition. Identifying and nurturing these relationships is essential for your well-being and recovery.

Firstly, when identifying trusted friends and family members, consider individuals who have consistently shown empathy, understanding, and non-judgmental support towards you. These are people who listen actively, validate your feelings, and offer practical help when needed. Trusted individuals may include close friends who have witnessed the dynamics of your relationship firsthand, family members who have always prioritized your welfare, or colleagues and mentors who have offered guidance and encouragement. Look for those who respect your autonomy and decisions, even if they may not fully understand the complexities of narcissistic abuse.

It is important to assess the reliability and trustworthiness of potential supporters. Consider whether they can maintain confidentiality about your plans to leave and respect your need for privacy. Confidentiality is crucial, especially if you fear that your narcissistic partner may attempt to interfere or retaliate against you or your support system. Choose individuals who have demonstrated discretion and can be trusted not to inadvertently disclose sensitive information.

When approaching trusted friends and family members about your situation, be prepared for varied reactions. Some may already have concerns about your well-being and be relieved that you are seeking help. Others may initially struggle to comprehend the complexities of narcissistic abuse or may find it difficult to accept that someone they know could behave in such manipulative ways. Provide information and resources that can help them understand the dynamics of narcissistic relationships and reassure them that their support is invaluable to your safety and recovery.

Communication is key when building a support system. Clearly articulate your needs and boundaries to your trusted individuals. Let them know how they can best support you—whether it's providing emotional encouragement, offering practical assistance with childcare or transportation, or simply being a listening ear during moments of distress. Establishing open and honest communication fosters a supportive environment where you feel safe expressing your feelings and seeking guidance without fear of judgment.

In some cases, you may need to educate your support network about narcissistic personality disorder (NPD) and the tactics used by narcissists to manipulate and control their victims. Narcissistic abuse is often subtle and difficult to detect from the outside, so helping your supporters understand the psychological and emotional impact can empower them to provide more effective support. Share resources such as articles, books, or reputable websites that explain narcissistic behavior and its effects on victims.

This education can also help your supporters recognize warning signs and respond appropriately if they observe concerning behavior from your partner.

Practical assistance from your support system can greatly facilitate your transition out of the relationship. This may include helping you gather important documents, pack essential belongings, and secure temporary housing or accommodation. Trusted friends and family members can also assist with logistical tasks such as arranging transportation, accompanying you to legal appointments or counseling sessions, and providing childcare or pet care during critical moments. Their practical support not only lightens the burden on you but also reinforces your sense of agency and capability as you navigate the complexities of leaving.

Emotional support is equally vital during this challenging time. Narcissistic abuse often leaves victims feeling isolated, invalidated, and emotionally drained. Your support system serves as a source of validation, empathy, and encouragement, reminding you that you are not alone in your journey. They can offer reassurance, affirm your strengths and resilience, and provide a safe space to process your emotions without fear of judgment. Regular check-ins and conversations with your supporters can help you stay grounded, maintain perspective, and bolster your determination to break free from the abusive relationship.

While friends and family members are crucial components of your support system, consider expanding your network to include professionals and organizations specializing in domestic abuse and trauma recovery.

Seek out local support groups, hotlines, or counseling services that offer specialized assistance to victims of narcissistic abuse. These resources can provide additional emotional support, practical guidance, and access to legal and financial resources that are instrumental in your journey towards safety and healing.

As you build and strengthen your support system, prioritize self-care and emotional resilience. Taking care of your physical, mental, and emotional well-being is essential for navigating the challenges of leaving a narcissistic relationship and rebuilding your life. Engage in activities that promote relaxation, such as yoga, meditation, or spending time in nature. Nurture hobbies and interests that bring you joy and fulfillment, reminding yourself of your worth and individuality outside of the abusive relationship.

Building a support system is a vital component of preparing to leave a narcissistic relationship. Identify trusted friends and family members who can offer emotional support, practical assistance, and validation during this challenging time. Communicate openly about your needs and boundaries, educate them about narcissistic abuse, and seek their assistance in gathering resources and navigating the logistical aspects of leaving. Their unwavering support and encouragement can provide the strength and reassurance you need to take decisive steps towards reclaiming your safety, autonomy, and emotional well-being.

Seeking professional help from therapists and support groups is a crucial step for individuals preparing to leave a narcissistic relationship.

These resources provide specialized support, guidance, and validation that are essential for navigating the complexities of narcissistic abuse, healing from emotional trauma, and rebuilding a healthy sense of self-worth and autonomy.

Therapists who specialize in trauma, domestic abuse, and narcissistic personality disorder (NPD) can offer invaluable support to victims. They provide a safe and confidential space to explore and process the emotional impact of narcissistic abuse, validate your experiences, and develop coping strategies to manage the trauma. A therapist can help you understand the dynamics of narcissistic relationships, recognize patterns of manipulation and control, and regain a sense of clarity and perspective. They can also assist in rebuilding your self-esteem, setting boundaries, and developing healthy relationship skills that empower you to establish fulfilling connections in the future.

Support groups tailored to survivors of narcissistic abuse offer a unique opportunity to connect with others who have experienced similar challenges and validate your feelings and experiences. These groups provide a supportive community where you can share your story, receive empathy and understanding, and gain insights from others who are on similar journeys. Hearing others' stories of survival and recovery can be empowering and reassuring, reminding you that you are not alone in your struggle. Support groups may also provide practical advice, resources, and strategies for coping with the aftermath of leaving a narcissistic relationship and rebuilding your life.

Both therapists and support groups play complementary roles in your healing journey.

While therapists offer individualized support and personalized guidance, support groups offer peer support and a sense of solidarity with others who understand your experience firsthand. Together, these resources create a comprehensive support network that addresses your emotional, psychological, and practical needs as you navigate the challenges of leaving a narcissistic partner and reclaiming your life.

When seeking professional help, it is important to find therapists and support groups that specialize in trauma and domestic abuse, particularly narcissistic abuse. Look for professionals who have experience working with survivors of narcissistic relationships and who create a safe and non-judgmental environment for healing. Consider scheduling initial consultations with therapists to ensure they are a good fit for your needs and goals. Similarly, explore different support groups to find one where you feel comfortable sharing your experiences and receiving support from peers.

Professional help can empower you to understand and process the complex emotions associated with narcissistic abuse, develop effective coping strategies, and rebuild your self-esteem and confidence. It provides a crucial foundation for healing and recovery, enabling you to break free from the cycle of abuse, regain control over your life, and build healthier, more fulfilling relationships in the future. By prioritizing your emotional well-being and seeking support from trained professionals and peers, you take an important step towards reclaiming your identity, independence, and emotional resilience after the trauma of narcissistic abuse.

Documenting abuse in a narcissistic relationship is a critical and empowering step for victims seeking validation, protection, and justice. This documentation involves keeping detailed records of incidents, behaviors, communications, and other relevant information that illustrate the patterns of manipulation, control, and harm inflicted by the narcissistic partner. The importance of thorough documentation cannot be overstated, particularly when considering legal proceedings such as obtaining a restraining order, pursuing divorce or custody arrangements, or seeking justice for criminal acts.

Keeping Records of Incidents

Keeping accurate records of incidents of abuse serves several purposes in understanding and addressing narcissistic abuse. Victims often experience a wide range of abusive behaviors, including emotional manipulation, verbal abuse, gaslighting, financial control, and sometimes physical violence. Documenting these incidents helps victims validate their experiences, as narcissists are adept at distorting reality and minimizing their abusive behaviors.

Types of Incidents to Document:

1. Verbal and Emotional Abuse: Record instances of insults, threats, intimidation, and demeaning comments made by the narcissistic partner. Note the date, time, location, and any witnesses present during these incidents.

2. Gaslighting and Manipulation: Document instances where the narcissist denies or distorts facts, dismisses your feelings, or undermines your perception of reality.

Gaslighting tactics are intended to confuse and control victims, making documentation crucial to maintaining clarity and perspective.

3. Financial Control: Keep records of financial transactions, control tactics, or restrictions imposed by the narcissistic partner. This may include withholding money, preventing access to financial resources, or sabotaging employment or financial independence.

4. Physical Abuse: If physical violence occurs, document injuries with photographs, medical reports, and any relevant documentation from law enforcement or healthcare professionals. Include details such as the circumstances leading to the incident and any threats or patterns of escalating violence.

5. Digital Abuse: In cases where the narcissistic partner engages in digital abuse, such as monitoring your communications, hacking accounts, or spreading false information online, document these incidents with screenshots, emails, or other electronic evidence.

Methods of Documentation:

1. Written Logs: Maintain a detailed written log or journal of abusive incidents, including dates, times, locations, descriptions of events, and your emotional reactions. This provides a chronological record of abuse patterns over time.

2. Audio or Video Recordings: In some jurisdictions, recording conversations with the consent of at least one party (depending on local laws) can provide evidence of abusive behaviors, threats, or manipulative tactics used by the narcissistic partner.

3. Photographic Evidence: Take photographs of injuries, damaged property, or physical evidence of abuse. Ensure these photos are dated and stored securely, as they may be crucial in legal proceedings.

4. Correspondence: Save copies of emails, text messages, social media posts, and other written communications that demonstrate abusive behaviors or threats. These communications can help corroborate your experiences and provide evidence of ongoing abuse.

5. Witness Statements: If possible, obtain statements from witnesses who have observed abusive behaviors or interactions with the narcissistic partner. Witness testimony can strengthen your case and validate your experiences in legal proceedings.

Importance of Documentation in Legal Proceedings

Documentation plays a pivotal role in legal proceedings involving narcissistic abuse, providing evidence to support claims of abuse, secure protective orders, and pursue justice. Courts rely on objective evidence to substantiate allegations of abuse and make informed decisions regarding the safety and welfare of victims and their dependents. The following are key aspects highlighting the significance of documentation in legal contexts:

1. Obtaining Protective Orders: Documentation of abusive incidents is crucial when seeking a protective order or restraining order against the narcissistic partner. Courts require evidence of imminent danger or past abuse to grant protective measures that safeguard victims from further harm. Detailed records of abusive behaviors, threats, and patterns of control provide compelling evidence supporting the need for legal protection.

2. Divorce and Custody Proceedings: In cases involving divorce or child custody disputes, documentation of narcissistic abuse is essential in presenting a clear and factual account of the dynamics within the relationship. Courts consider evidence of abuse when making decisions about custody arrangements, visitation rights, and the division of assets. Documentation helps demonstrate the narcissistic partner's capacity to inflict harm, manipulate situations, and undermine the best interests of children or vulnerable family members.

3. Criminal Proceedings: In situations where abuse escalates to criminal acts, such as physical assault, stalking, harassment, or financial exploitation, documentation serves as critical evidence in criminal investigations and prosecutions. Law enforcement agencies rely on detailed records, witness statements, and physical evidence to hold perpetrators accountable for their actions and ensure justice for victims.

4. Establishing Patterns of Behavior: Documentation allows victims to establish patterns of abusive behavior over time, demonstrating the consistency and severity of abuse perpetrated by the narcissistic partner.

This longitudinal perspective provides a comprehensive understanding of the impact of abuse on victims' lives and underscores the need for legal intervention and protection.

5. Protecting Legal Rights: Documenting abuse empowers victims to assert their legal rights and advocate for their safety and well-being in legal proceedings. It provides a factual basis for legal arguments, supports requests for temporary or permanent protective measures, and strengthens claims for compensation or restitution in cases of financial or emotional harm.

6. Counteracting Gaslighting and Denial: Narcissists often use gaslighting tactics to undermine victims' credibility and distort the truth. Detailed documentation of abusive incidents counteracts gaslighting by providing concrete evidence of abusive behaviors and validating victims' experiences. It ensures that victims' voices are heard and their accounts are taken seriously in legal settings.

Documenting abuse in a narcissistic relationship is a proactive and empowering strategy for victims seeking validation, protection, and legal recourse. By keeping thorough records of abusive incidents, behaviors, communications, and other relevant information, victims can substantiate their experiences, establish patterns of abuse, and strengthen their position in legal proceedings. Documentation serves as a critical tool for obtaining protective orders, navigating divorce and custody disputes, supporting criminal prosecutions, and asserting legal rights. It empowers victims to break free from cycles of abuse, reclaim their autonomy, and pursue justice and healing on their terms.

"You will never really see how toxic someone is until
you breathe fresher air."

Chapter 3: Practical Tactics for Disengagement

The Grey Rock Method

The Grey Rock Method is a strategy designed to help individuals disengage from interactions with narcissistic or toxic individuals by making themselves as uninteresting and unresponsive as possible. This technique is particularly useful for those who are unable to completely cut ties with the narcissist, such as in cases of co-parenting, shared workplaces, or when preparing to leave the relationship. By employing the Grey Rock Method, victims aim to minimize the emotional impact and attention they provide to the narcissist, thereby reducing the narcissist's ability to manipulate or control them.

What It Is and How to Use It Effectively

The Grey Rock Method derives its name from the idea of becoming as dull and unremarkable as a grey rock. The core principle involves limiting emotional reactions, avoiding engagement in drama, and maintaining a neutral demeanor during interactions with the narcissist. This technique works on the premise that narcissists thrive on attention, emotional responses, and drama; by depriving them of these, the narcissist loses interest and their manipulative efforts become less effective.

Implementing the Grey Rock Method involves several key strategies:

1. Neutral Responses: When interacting with the narcissist, respond in a neutral, detached manner.

Avoid showing any strong emotions, whether positive or negative. Use simple, short responses such as "yes," "no," or "I don't know." Refrain from elaborating or engaging in deeper conversation, which can provide the narcissist with opportunities to manipulate or provoke you.

2. Avoiding Drama: Do not engage in arguments, debates, or emotional confrontations. Narcissists often create conflict to elicit emotional reactions. By refusing to participate in these dramas, you deny them the satisfaction they seek. If the narcissist attempts to provoke you, remain calm and non-reactive, and remove yourself from the situation if necessary.

3. Minimal Interaction: Limit interactions with the narcissist to what is absolutely necessary. If you share a living space or work environment, find ways to minimize contact, such as by spending time in different rooms or areas, or by scheduling activities to avoid overlap. Communicate only about essential topics and keep conversations brief and to the point.

4. Non-Engagement: Avoid sharing personal information, opinions, or feelings with the narcissist. They may use this information against you or to manipulate you. Stick to factual, impersonal topics, and steer the conversation away from yourself whenever possible.

5. Monotone Communication: When speaking with the narcissist, use a monotone voice. This helps to convey disinterest and makes it harder for the narcissist to gauge your emotional state. The less expressive you are, the less material they have to manipulate.

6. Consistent Boundaries: Set and maintain clear boundaries regarding acceptable behavior and communication. Consistently enforce these boundaries without explanation or justification. For example, if the narcissist starts a conversation that crosses a boundary, calmly and firmly end the interaction or walk away.

Effectiveness of the Grey Rock Method relies on consistency and practice.** Here are some additional considerations for using the method effectively:

- Mental Preparation: Prepare yourself mentally for interactions with the narcissist. Remind yourself of your goal to remain unemotional and disengaged. Practice deep breathing or mindfulness techniques to stay calm and focused.

- Support System: Lean on your support system of trusted friends, family, or a therapist. They can provide emotional support and validation, helping you stay strong and consistent in your use of the Grey Rock Method.

- Self-Care: Prioritize self-care to maintain your emotional well-being. Engaging in activities that bring you joy, relaxation, and fulfillment can help offset the emotional toll of dealing with a narcissist.

Real-Life Examples and Scenarios

To better understand the Grey Rock Method, let's explore some real-life examples and scenarios illustrating its application.

Example 1: Co-Parenting with a Narcissist

Sarah shares custody of her children with her narcissistic ex-husband, Tom. Tom frequently tries to provoke Sarah by criticizing her parenting and making unreasonable demands. Instead of reacting emotionally or defending herself, Sarah uses the Grey Rock Method. During exchanges, she keeps her responses brief and factual. When Tom criticizes her, she simply says, "I understand your concern," without further elaboration. By maintaining a calm and neutral demeanor, Sarah denies Tom the emotional reaction he seeks. Over time, Tom's attempts to provoke her diminish as he realizes he no longer gets the desired response.

Example 2: Workplace Narcissist

John works with a colleague, Lisa, who exhibits narcissistic behaviors. Lisa often tries to undermine John and provoke him during meetings. John decides to implement the Grey Rock Method. In meetings, he keeps his contributions minimal and to the point. When Lisa makes provocative comments, John responds with neutral statements like, "I see," or "Noted." He avoids engaging in arguments or defending himself. By consistently using the Grey Rock Method, John reduces Lisa's ability to disrupt his work and protect his professional well-being.

Example 3: Family Gatherings

Emily has a narcissistic sibling, Mark, who frequently tries to dominate family gatherings with drama and conflict. Emily decides to use the Grey Rock Method to manage her interactions with Mark.

During family events, she engages minimally with him, sticking to superficial topics like the weather or shared memories. When Mark attempts to draw her into conflicts or provoke her, Emily responds with neutral comments and shifts her attention to other family members. By refusing to engage in Mark's antics, Emily preserves her peace and enjoys the family gathering without unnecessary stress.

Example 4: Digital Communication

David is in the process of leaving his narcissistic partner, Jane, but still has to communicate with her about logistical matters. Jane frequently sends provocative texts and emails trying to draw David into arguments. David uses the Grey Rock Method in his digital communication. He keeps his responses brief and factual, avoiding any emotional language. For example, when Jane sends a provocative message, David replies with a simple, "I will handle it," without further explanation or engagement. By maintaining a neutral tone, David reduces the emotional impact of Jane's messages and protects his mental well-being.

Example 5: Social Events

Rachel attends social events where her narcissistic friend, Chris, is often present. Chris likes to draw attention to himself by creating drama and provoking Rachel. To use the Grey Rock Method, Rachel minimizes her interactions with Chris. When Chris approaches her, she responds politely but briefly, without engaging in deep conversation. She avoids reacting to his provocative comments and instead redirects her attention to other friends or activities. By being uninteresting and unresponsive, Rachel limits Chris's ability to draw her into his drama.

Challenges and Considerations:

Implementing the Grey Rock Method can be challenging, especially in emotionally charged situations. Here are some considerations to keep in mind:

- Emotional Toll: Consistently suppressing your emotional responses can be exhausting and may take a toll on your mental health. It's important to find healthy outlets for your emotions, such as talking to a therapist, journaling, or engaging in self-care activities.

- Safety Concerns: In situations where there is a risk of physical violence, the Grey Rock Method may not be sufficient to ensure safety. Always prioritize your physical safety and seek help from law enforcement or domestic violence organizations if necessary.

- Consistency is Key: The effectiveness of the Grey Rock Method relies on consistency. Any deviation or emotional reaction can encourage the narcissist to continue their manipulative behaviors. Stay committed to the technique, even when it feels challenging.

- Not a Long-Term Solution: The Grey Rock Method is a short-term strategy for managing interactions with a narcissist. It is not a long-term solution for healing from abuse or rebuilding your life. Use this method as a tool while you work towards more permanent changes, such as leaving the relationship or establishing healthier boundaries.

- Personal Boundaries: Maintaining personal boundaries is crucial when using the Grey Rock Method.

Clearly define what behaviors you will and will not tolerate and enforce these boundaries consistently. This reinforces your commitment to disengaging from the narcissist's manipulation.

The Grey Rock Method is an effective strategy for disengaging from a narcissistic or toxic individual by making yourself uninteresting and unresponsive. By employing neutral responses, avoiding drama, minimizing interaction, and maintaining consistent boundaries, you can reduce the narcissist's ability to manipulate and control you. Real-life examples illustrate how this method can be applied in various situations, such as co-parenting, workplace interactions, family gatherings, digital communication, and social events. While the Grey Rock Method can be challenging to implement consistently, it offers a practical approach to managing interactions with a narcissist and protecting your emotional well-being. It is important to recognize that this method is a temporary strategy and should be used in conjunction with other steps towards healing and recovery, such as seeking professional support and establishing healthier, more fulfilling relationships.

No Contact Rule

The No Contact Rule is a crucial strategy for individuals seeking to heal from the emotional and psychological wounds inflicted by a narcissistic relationship. This approach involves cutting off all forms of communication and interaction with the narcissist, thereby eliminating the source of manipulation, control, and emotional abuse. The No Contact Rule is not just about physical separation; it extends to all modes of communication, including phone calls, text messages, emails, social media interactions, and indirect contact through mutual acquaintances. The importance of this rule lies in its ability to create a safe and supportive environment for healing, breaking the cycle of abuse, and fostering personal growth and recovery.

Importance of Cutting Off All Communication

Cutting off all communication with a narcissist is essential for several reasons. Firstly, narcissists thrive on control and manipulation. They use communication as a tool to maintain their influence over their victims, often employing tactics such as gaslighting, emotional blackmail, and intermittent reinforcement. By completely severing communication, victims remove the narcissist's ability to continue these manipulative behaviors. This creates a space where victims can begin to regain their sense of autonomy and self-worth, free from the constant emotional turmoil and psychological games.

Secondly, maintaining contact with a narcissist hinders the healing process. Every interaction, no matter how seemingly benign, has the potential to reopen emotional wounds and trigger traumatic memories.

Narcissists are adept at using even casual communication to reassert their dominance and destabilize their victims. By enforcing the No Contact Rule, individuals protect themselves from these recurring emotional assaults, allowing for a more focused and uninterrupted healing journey.

Moreover, cutting off communication is a powerful statement of self-respect and boundaries. It signifies a refusal to tolerate further abuse and a commitment to self-care and personal growth. For many victims, this is a vital step in reclaiming their identity and rebuilding their lives. It reinforces the message that their well-being is paramount and that they deserve to be treated with dignity and respect. This empowerment is crucial for long-term recovery and the establishment of healthier relationships in the future.

The No Contact Rule also helps break the cycle of trauma bonding. Trauma bonding occurs when victims develop an unhealthy attachment to their abuser due to intermittent reinforcement of affection and abuse. This bond is reinforced through sporadic positive interactions that follow periods of mistreatment, creating a confusing and damaging dynamic. By eliminating all contact, victims can break free from this cycle, reducing the psychological grip the narcissist holds over them and allowing for the formation of healthier, more stable emotional connections.

Dealing with Challenges and Maintaining Resolve

Implementing and maintaining the No Contact Rule can be incredibly challenging, especially in the initial stages.

The emotional and psychological ties to the narcissist can be strong, and the fear of retaliation or guilt can make it difficult to stay firm in the decision. However, understanding and preparing for these challenges can significantly enhance the likelihood of successfully maintaining no contact.

One of the primary challenges is the narcissist's reaction to the enforcement of no contact. Narcissists are likely to respond with a range of tactics designed to re-establish control. These can include love bombing, where the narcissist showers the victim with affection and promises of change to lure them back into the relationship. Alternatively, they might use intimidation, threats, or guilt-tripping to provoke a response. Understanding these tactics and being prepared for them is crucial. Recognize that these behaviors are manipulative strategies aimed at regaining control and that responding to them only perpetuates the cycle of abuse.

Another significant challenge is the emotional withdrawal symptoms that often accompany the enforcement of no contact. Victims may experience feelings of loneliness, guilt, or doubt. The emotional attachment to the narcissist, compounded by the manipulative tactics used during the relationship, can make the absence of communication feel overwhelming. It is important to acknowledge these feelings as a natural part of the healing process. Seeking support from trusted friends, family, or a therapist can provide the emotional reinforcement needed to stay committed to no contact.

Maintaining resolve also requires practical steps to prevent accidental or intentional breaches of no contact.

This includes blocking the narcissist's phone number, email address, and social media accounts. It may also involve informing mutual acquaintances about the decision and requesting that they do not relay any messages or information between you and the narcissist. In some cases, changing phone numbers, email addresses, or even moving to a new location may be necessary to ensure complete separation.

Building a strong support system is crucial for maintaining no contact. Surrounding yourself with people who understand your situation and can offer emotional support and encouragement is invaluable. Support groups, whether in-person or online, can provide a sense of community and shared experience, reducing feelings of isolation and reinforcing the importance of no contact. Additionally, professional support from therapists or counselors who specialize in narcissistic abuse can offer personalized strategies and coping mechanisms to navigate the challenges of no contact.

Focusing on personal growth and self-care is another effective way to maintain resolve. Engage in activities that promote physical, emotional, and mental well-being. This can include hobbies, exercise, meditation, or pursuing new interests and goals. Rebuilding your life and identity outside of the narcissistic relationship fosters a sense of empowerment and self-worth, making it easier to stay committed to no contact. Journaling can also be a therapeutic tool, helping to process emotions and track progress in your healing journey.

Setting clear goals and reminders can help maintain focus and resolve.

Remind yourself regularly of the reasons for enforcing no contact and the benefits it brings to your life. Writing down these reasons and revisiting them during moments of doubt can reinforce your commitment. Visualizing a future free from the narcissist's influence, where you are empowered, happy, and healthy, can also serve as a powerful motivator.

The No Contact Rule is a vital strategy for breaking free from a narcissistic relationship and embarking on a path of healing and recovery. By cutting off all communication, victims protect themselves from further manipulation and emotional abuse, allowing for the restoration of their sense of self and autonomy. The challenges of implementing and maintaining no contact are significant but can be navigated with preparation, support, and a focus on personal growth. Through the No Contact Rule, individuals can reclaim their lives, build healthier relationships, and achieve lasting recovery from narcissistic abuse.

Setting Boundaries

Setting boundaries is an essential skill for anyone recovering from a relationship with a narcissist. Boundaries serve as protective barriers that define personal space, values, and limits, allowing individuals to reclaim their autonomy and build healthier relationships. This chapter delves into the intricacies of establishing and enforcing boundaries and provides strategies for communicating them assertively.

How to Establish and Enforce Boundaries

Establishing boundaries starts with self-awareness. This involves understanding one's own needs, values, and limits. It requires a deep reflection on past experiences, especially those involving the narcissist, to identify what behaviors and situations have been harmful or uncomfortable. This self-reflection is a critical first step in recognizing where boundaries need to be set. For instance, if constant criticism from the narcissist has eroded self-esteem, it becomes clear that a boundary around respectful communication is necessary.

Once personal boundaries are identified, the next step is to articulate them clearly and specifically. Ambiguity can lead to misunderstandings and weaken the effectiveness of the boundaries. For example, instead of saying, "I need more respect," it is more effective to state, "I need you to speak to me without raising your voice or calling me names." Specificity helps in communicating the exact behavior that is unacceptable and what the expected behavior should be.

Enforcing boundaries is equally important as establishing them. This requires consistency and follow-through. When a boundary is crossed, it is crucial to address the violation immediately. This might involve reminding the person of the boundary and the consequences of violating it. For instance, if a boundary around phone calls has been set to avoid late-night disturbances, and the narcissist calls late at night, enforcing the boundary might involve not answering the call and addressing the issue the next day by reiterating the boundary and its importance.

Another key aspect of enforcing boundaries is to ensure that consequences are fair and consistent. Consequences should be proportionate to the violation and should reinforce the importance of the boundary. If boundaries are repeatedly violated despite reminders, it might be necessary to escalate the consequences. This could range from reducing contact with the narcissist to completely severing ties if the violations are severe and persistent.

Maintaining boundaries also requires internal strength and resilience. The narcissist may react negatively to boundaries, using tactics such as guilt-tripping, gaslighting, or even anger to push back against them. It is important to stay firm and not be swayed by these manipulative tactics. This might involve seeking support from friends, family, or a therapist who can provide encouragement and reinforcement.

Practicing self-care is vital when establishing and enforcing boundaries. Setting boundaries can be emotionally draining, especially when dealing with a narcissist who might not respect them.

Engaging in activities that promote mental and emotional well-being, such as exercise, meditation, or hobbies, can help in maintaining the strength needed to uphold boundaries.

Documenting boundaries and any incidents of their violation can also be helpful. Keeping a record provides clarity and a sense of control. It can also be useful if there is a need to explain the situation to a third party, such as a therapist or legal professional.

Communicating Boundaries Assertively

Assertive communication is key to effectively setting and maintaining boundaries. It involves expressing thoughts and needs clearly, directly, and respectfully, without being passive or aggressive. For individuals recovering from a relationship with a narcissist, developing assertive communication skills can be particularly empowering.

To communicate boundaries assertively, start by using "I" statements. "I" statements focus on your own feelings and needs, rather than placing blame on the other person. For example, instead of saying, "You never listen to me," you might say, "I feel unheard when my opinions are dismissed." This approach reduces defensiveness and opens up a dialogue.

Clarity and brevity are also important in assertive communication. Be concise and to the point, ensuring that your message is understood. Avoid over-explaining or justifying your boundaries, as this can dilute the message and give the impression that the boundary is negotiable.

For instance, "I need personal space when I come home from work to unwind" is clear and direct.

Non-verbal communication plays a significant role in how boundaries are perceived. Maintain eye contact, use a calm and steady tone of voice, and ensure your body language is open and assertive. Avoid crossing your arms or looking away, as these can be interpreted as signs of weakness or uncertainty.

Timing is also crucial when communicating boundaries. Choose a time when both parties are calm and not in the midst of an argument. This increases the likelihood that your message will be heard and respected. For example, instead of bringing up a boundary issue during a heated argument, wait until a more neutral time to discuss your needs.

Practice active listening when communicating boundaries. This means fully concentrating on what the other person is saying, without interrupting or planning your response while they are speaking. Active listening demonstrates respect and can de-escalate potential conflicts. It also provides an opportunity to understand the other person's perspective, which can be important in negotiating boundaries.

It is important to anticipate resistance and prepare for it. Narcissists, in particular, are likely to challenge boundaries and may use manipulative tactics to undermine them. Be prepared to stand your ground and repeat your boundary as many times as necessary. Repetition reinforces the seriousness of your boundary and demonstrates your commitment to it.

Using assertive communication can be challenging at first, especially for individuals who have not been accustomed to it. Practicing with a trusted friend or therapist can be beneficial. Role-playing scenarios where you practice setting and enforcing boundaries can build confidence and improve your assertiveness skills.

Empathy can also play a role in assertive communication. While it is crucial to be firm, showing empathy can help in maintaining a respectful tone. For example, acknowledging the other person's feelings with a statement like, "I understand that this might be difficult for you, but it is important for me to have this boundary," can convey respect while still asserting your needs.

Setting and enforcing boundaries with a narcissist is a continuous process that requires vigilance and adaptation. As circumstances change and as you grow in your recovery, your boundaries may need to be adjusted. Regularly reviewing and reassessing your boundaries ensures that they remain relevant and effective.

Setting boundaries is a vital step in breaking free from a narcissist and reclaiming your autonomy. It involves a thorough understanding of your own needs and limits, clear and specific communication, and consistent enforcement. Assertive communication is essential in conveying your boundaries effectively and ensuring they are respected. By developing these skills and maintaining resilience, you can create a safer and more respectful environment for yourself, paving the way for healthier relationships and personal well-being.

Managing Emotional Triggers

Emotional triggers are stimuli that provoke strong emotional responses, often linked to past experiences, particularly traumatic ones. For individuals recovering from a relationship with a narcissist, managing emotional triggers is a crucial part of the healing process. Emotional triggers can disrupt daily life, cause distress, and hinder recovery. In this section, we will explore techniques for staying calm and composed, along with mindfulness and stress management strategies to help you navigate and manage these emotional responses effectively.

Techniques for Staying Calm and Composed

Staying calm and composed in the face of emotional triggers requires a combination of self-awareness, practical techniques, and consistent practice. One of the first steps is to identify your triggers. Understanding what specific situations, words, or behaviors provoke strong emotional reactions can help you prepare and respond more effectively. Keeping a journal to track these triggers and your responses to them can provide valuable insights and help in developing coping strategies.

One effective technique for staying calm is controlled breathing. When faced with a trigger, the body often goes into a fight-or-flight mode, characterized by rapid, shallow breathing. This response can exacerbate feelings of anxiety and panic. Practicing deep, diaphragmatic breathing can help counteract this response.

For instance, the 4-7-8 breathing technique involves inhaling deeply through the nose for a count of four, holding the breath for a count of seven, and exhaling slowly through the mouth for a count of eight. This method can help slow down your heart rate and promote a sense of calm.

Progressive muscle relaxation (PMR) is another useful technique. PMR involves tensing and then slowly relaxing different muscle groups in the body, starting from the toes and working up to the head. This process can help reduce physical tension and promote relaxation. By focusing on the physical act of tensing and relaxing muscles, you can also distract your mind from the emotional trigger and bring your focus back to your body.

Grounding techniques can also be effective in managing emotional triggers. Grounding involves using the five senses to bring your focus to the present moment, helping to disrupt the cycle of distressing thoughts. For example, the 5-4-3-2-1 technique involves identifying five things you can see, four things you can touch, three things you can hear, two things you can smell, and one thing you can taste. This technique can help anchor you in the present moment and reduce the intensity of emotional reactions.

Visualization and guided imagery can also be powerful tools for staying calm. Visualization involves creating a mental image of a peaceful and safe place, such as a beach, forest, or any other setting that brings you comfort. By focusing on the details of this image—such as the sounds, smells, and sensations—you can create a mental escape from the triggering situation.

Guided imagery, often facilitated by a therapist or through audio recordings, can help you navigate this process more effectively.

Engaging in physical activity is another effective way to manage emotional triggers. Exercise releases endorphins, which are natural mood lifters, and can help reduce stress and anxiety. Activities such as walking, jogging, yoga, or even dancing can provide a physical outlet for the built-up tension and help restore a sense of calm. Regular physical activity also promotes overall mental and emotional well-being, making it easier to handle stressors and triggers when they arise.

Developing a personal mantra or affirmation can also be beneficial. A mantra is a word or phrase that you repeat to yourself to provide comfort and focus. For example, repeating phrases like "I am safe," "This too shall pass," or "I am in control of my response" can help counteract negative thoughts and emotions triggered by past experiences. These affirmations can serve as reminders of your strength and resilience, helping you stay composed in the face of emotional challenges.

Mindfulness and Stress Management Strategies

Mindfulness is the practice of bringing one's attention to the present moment in a non-judgmental way. It can be a powerful tool in managing emotional triggers and reducing stress. Mindfulness practices help individuals become more aware of their thoughts and feelings without becoming overwhelmed by them. This heightened awareness can lead to better emotional regulation and a greater sense of control.

One of the most well-known mindfulness practices is mindfulness meditation. This involves sitting quietly and focusing on your breath, a word or phrase, or a specific thought, while gently bringing your mind back to the focus point whenever it wanders. Even short daily sessions of mindfulness meditation can lead to significant improvements in emotional regulation and stress management. Apps like Headspace and Calm offer guided meditations that can be helpful for beginners.

Mindful breathing is another effective strategy. This practice involves paying close attention to the process of breathing. You might focus on the sensation of air entering and leaving your nostrils, the rise and fall of your chest, or the feeling of your breath in your abdomen. Whenever your mind starts to wander, gently bring your attention back to your breath. This practice can be particularly useful during moments of emotional distress, as it helps ground you in the present moment and reduce anxiety.

Body scan meditation is a mindfulness practice that involves mentally scanning your body from head to toe, paying attention to any sensations, tension, or discomfort. This practice helps you become more aware of how stress and emotions manifest in your body. By recognizing these physical signs, you can address them more effectively, whether through relaxation techniques or other forms of self-care.

Mindful walking is a form of mindfulness that involves focusing on the experience of walking. This can be done indoors or outdoors, paying attention to the sensation of your feet touching the ground, the movement of your legs, and the rhythm of your breath.

Mindful walking combines the benefits of physical activity with mindfulness, making it an excellent practice for managing stress and emotional triggers.

In addition to mindfulness practices, incorporating stress management strategies into your daily routine can help build resilience against emotional triggers. One such strategy is time management. Poor time management can lead to unnecessary stress, making you more susceptible to emotional triggers. Prioritizing tasks, breaking them down into manageable steps, and setting realistic deadlines can help reduce stress and improve your ability to handle challenging situations.

Creating a balanced lifestyle is also crucial. This includes maintaining a healthy diet, getting regular exercise, ensuring adequate sleep, and engaging in activities that you enjoy and find fulfilling. A balanced lifestyle supports overall mental and emotional health, making it easier to cope with stress and emotional triggers when they arise.

Social support is another important aspect of stress management. Building and maintaining strong relationships with friends, family, and support groups can provide a valuable network of support. Talking about your experiences and feelings with trusted individuals can help you process emotions and gain different perspectives. Support groups, particularly those focused on recovering from narcissistic relationships, can provide a sense of community and understanding that is particularly beneficial.

Another effective stress management strategy is cognitive restructuring, which involves changing negative thought patterns. This technique is often used in cognitive-behavioral therapy (CBT) and involves identifying irrational or harmful thoughts, challenging them, and replacing them with more balanced and realistic ones. For instance, if you find yourself thinking, "I can't handle this," you might challenge this thought by reminding yourself of times when you have successfully managed similar situations, thereby shifting your mindset to, "I have handled difficult situations before, and I can handle this too."

Creative activities can also serve as powerful stress management tools. Engaging in hobbies such as painting, writing, playing music, or crafting can provide an emotional outlet and help reduce stress. These activities allow for self-expression and can be particularly therapeutic, helping to process emotions in a healthy and constructive way.

Lastly, developing a self-care routine tailored to your needs can significantly impact your ability to manage stress and emotional triggers. Self-care involves taking deliberate actions to care for your mental, emotional, and physical health. This might include activities like taking a relaxing bath, reading a book, spending time in nature, practicing yoga, or even indulging in a favorite treat. The key is to find activities that nourish you and incorporate them regularly into your routine.

Managing emotional triggers involves a combination of techniques for staying calm and composed, mindfulness practices, and comprehensive stress management strategies.

By identifying your triggers, practicing controlled breathing, engaging in physical activity, and employing mindfulness techniques, you can better navigate and manage your emotional responses. Building a balanced lifestyle, seeking social support, and incorporating creative activities and self-care into your routine are also essential components in maintaining emotional well-being and resilience. Through consistent practice and self-awareness, you can develop the skills needed to effectively manage emotional triggers and foster a healthier, more balanced life.

"Trying to reason with a narcissist is like trying to nail
Jello to a tree."

Understanding Your Rights

Navigating the aftermath of a relationship with a narcissist often involves complex legal and financial considerations. Understanding your rights and the legal options available to you is crucial for ensuring your protection and achieving a fair resolution. This section delves into the legal options and protections available, and the importance of seeking legal advice and representation.

Legal Options and Protections Available

When disentangling from a relationship with a narcissist, particularly if the relationship involves marriage, children, or shared assets, the legal landscape can be daunting. However, there are numerous legal protections and options designed to safeguard your interests.

One of the most critical steps is understanding the various types of abuse and the legal remedies available for each. Abuse can be physical, emotional, psychological, financial, or a combination of these. Each type of abuse has specific legal frameworks and protections. For instance, physical abuse is often addressed under criminal law, with restraining orders and protective orders serving as immediate legal remedies to ensure the victim's safety. These orders can prevent the abuser from contacting or approaching the victim, offering a crucial layer of protection.

Emotional and psychological abuse, while more challenging to prove, can also be addressed legally. Harassment, stalking, and coercive control are behaviors that many jurisdictions recognize as criminal acts. Documenting these forms of abuse through detailed records, witness statements, and evidence such as emails or messages can strengthen your case. Legal options for emotional abuse often include protective orders and, in some cases, criminal charges against the abuser.

Financial abuse, which involves controlling a victim's access to financial resources, can be particularly insidious. This form of abuse can leave victims without the means to support themselves or their children, creating significant barriers to leaving the abusive relationship. Legal remedies for financial abuse include court-ordered spousal support, child support, and the equitable division of marital assets. In some cases, courts may order restitution for misappropriated funds or assets.

For those married to a narcissist, divorce is often the primary legal option to sever ties. Divorce laws vary by jurisdiction, but common grounds for divorce include irreconcilable differences, adultery, and cruelty. In cases involving narcissistic abuse, proving cruelty can be particularly relevant. It is essential to gather comprehensive evidence of the abuse, including medical records, police reports, and witness testimonies, to support your claims.

Child custody is another significant legal consideration. Narcissistic individuals may use children as pawns to maintain control and inflict further harm on their ex-partner.

Courts prioritize the best interests of the child in custody cases, considering factors such as the child's safety, stability, and well-being. Demonstrating the narcissist's harmful behavior and its impact on the children is crucial. This can involve presenting evidence of neglect, emotional abuse, or any behavior that jeopardizes the child's welfare. Supervised visitation or limited custody may be appropriate in cases where the narcissist poses a risk to the children.

Another critical legal aspect is property and asset division. Narcissists often manipulate financial matters to their advantage, hiding assets or using marital funds for personal gain. In many jurisdictions, marital property is subject to equitable distribution, meaning it is divided fairly, though not necessarily equally. Forensic accountants can play a vital role in uncovering hidden assets and ensuring a fair division. Ensuring all financial documentation is thorough and accurate is essential to prevent the narcissist from exploiting the situation.

Employment and workplace protections are also relevant, especially if the narcissist is a co-worker or superior. Many jurisdictions have laws protecting employees from harassment and discrimination. Filing a complaint with the human resources department or relevant employment tribunal can initiate an investigation into the narcissist's behavior. Legal protections may also include anti-retaliation provisions to safeguard the victim from further harm.

Housing protections can be critical for those who live with their abuser.

Laws such as the Violence Against Women Act (VAWA) in the United States provide protections for victims of domestic violence, including the right to change locks, early lease termination, and relocation assistance. Understanding these rights can help secure safe and stable housing away from the abuser.

Navigating the intersection of criminal and civil law is often necessary in cases of severe abuse. Criminal charges can be pursued for assault, harassment, stalking, and other illegal behaviors, providing immediate protection through arrest and prosecution. Civil remedies, such as restraining orders, can complement criminal proceedings by offering longer-term protection and specific prohibitions against contact or proximity.

Seeking legal advice early in the process is crucial to understand the full spectrum of options and protections available. Legal professionals can provide tailored advice based on the specifics of your situation, ensuring that your rights are fully protected.

Seeking Legal Advice and Representation

Seeking legal advice and representation is a critical step in protecting your rights and navigating the legal complexities involved in escaping a narcissistic relationship. Legal professionals can offer invaluable guidance, support, and advocacy throughout the process.

One of the first steps in seeking legal advice is finding the right attorney. Look for attorneys who specialize in family law, domestic violence, or related fields.

Specialization ensures that the attorney is well-versed in the nuances of these cases and can provide the most effective representation. Personal referrals from trusted friends or professionals can be helpful, as can resources from local domestic violence organizations, which often have lists of recommended attorneys.

Initial consultations with attorneys are typically free and provide an opportunity to discuss your case and assess the attorney's suitability. Prepare for these consultations by gathering all relevant documentation, including evidence of abuse, financial records, and any previous legal actions taken. Clearly outline your objectives, such as obtaining a restraining order, filing for divorce, or securing custody of children.

During the consultation, evaluate the attorney's experience, communication style, and approach to your case. It is crucial to feel comfortable and confident in your attorney's ability to represent you effectively. Ask about their experience with similar cases, their strategy for handling your case, and their availability for communication and updates.

Cost is another important consideration. Legal representation can be expensive, and understanding the fee structure upfront is essential. Some attorneys charge hourly rates, while others may offer flat fees for specific services. In some cases, payment plans or sliding scale fees based on income may be available. Additionally, some nonprofit organizations and legal aid societies offer free or low-cost legal services for victims of domestic abuse.

Legal representation is particularly crucial when dealing with a narcissist, who is likely to use manipulative tactics in legal proceedings. An experienced attorney can anticipate these tactics and counter them effectively. For example, narcissists often use the court system as a tool of harassment, filing frivolous motions or dragging out proceedings to exhaust their victim emotionally and financially. A skilled attorney can identify these tactics and work to minimize their impact, potentially seeking sanctions against the narcissist for abusive litigation practices.

Attorneys can also help in securing protective orders, which are essential for ensuring safety and peace of mind. Protective orders, also known as restraining orders, legally prohibit the abuser from contacting or approaching the victim. Violations of these orders can result in immediate legal consequences, including arrest. Attorneys can assist in filing for these orders, presenting evidence to the court, and advocating for the terms necessary to protect the victim and any children involved.

In cases of divorce, legal representation is crucial for navigating the complexities of property division, spousal support, and custody arrangements. An attorney can help ensure that the divorce settlement is fair and that the narcissist does not exploit the process to their advantage. For example, they can work with forensic accountants to uncover hidden assets and advocate for equitable division of property. They can also negotiate spousal support to ensure financial stability post-divorce.

Child custody disputes involving a narcissist can be particularly challenging.

Narcissists may use manipulative tactics to gain custody or control over the children, not out of genuine concern for their well-being, but as a means to continue exerting power over their ex-partner. An attorney can advocate for the best interests of the children, presenting evidence of the narcissist's harmful behavior and its impact on the children. They can also help in setting up custody arrangements that protect the children and provide stability.

Legal representation is also essential for addressing financial abuse. Attorneys can help secure spousal support and child support, ensuring that the victim has the financial resources needed to rebuild their life. They can also assist in recovering funds or assets that the narcissist may have misappropriated. In some cases, they may work with financial experts to assess the full extent of the financial abuse and seek restitution.

In addition to direct legal representation, attorneys can provide referrals to other professionals who may be necessary for your case. This might include mental health professionals, financial advisors, or social workers who can offer additional support and resources.

Beyond the courtroom, legal professionals can advocate for broader systemic changes to protect victims of narcissistic abuse. This might involve lobbying for stronger domestic violence laws, better enforcement of existing protections, or more resources for victims. By working with advocacy organizations, attorneys can help drive changes that benefit all victims of abuse, not just their individual clients.

Understanding your legal rights and seeking competent legal advice and representation are critical steps in escaping a narcissistic relationship and protecting your future. Legal professionals provide essential support and advocacy, helping to navigate the complexities of the legal system and ensuring that your rights are protected. By taking proactive steps to secure legal representation, you can achieve a fair resolution and build a safer, more stable future for yourself and your children.

Protecting Your Assets

In the aftermath of a relationship with a narcissist, one of the most critical concerns is protecting your assets. Narcissists often exert control over finances as a means of manipulation and power. This can leave victims vulnerable and financially unstable. This section will explore financial planning and securing assets, as well as steps to take if the narcissist controls the finances.

Financial Planning and Securing Assets

Financial planning is an essential step in reclaiming control over your life and ensuring financial stability. It involves assessing your current financial situation, setting short- and long-term financial goals, and implementing strategies to achieve those goals.

The first step in financial planning is to take a comprehensive inventory of your assets and liabilities. This includes documenting all bank accounts, investment accounts, retirement funds, real estate holdings, personal property, and any other assets.

Simultaneously, list all liabilities such as mortgages, loans, credit card debt, and any other financial obligations. Having a clear picture of your financial standing is crucial for making informed decisions.

Next, it is essential to secure your financial records. Narcissists may attempt to access or manipulate these records to their advantage. Ensure that all financial documents are stored in a secure location, such as a safe deposit box or a secure digital storage service. Change passwords for online accounts and consider setting up two-factor authentication to enhance security.

Creating a budget is a vital component of financial planning. A budget helps track income and expenses, identify unnecessary expenditures, and allocate funds towards savings and debt repayment. Start by listing all sources of income and categorizing expenses into fixed (e.g., rent, utilities) and variable (e.g., groceries, entertainment) categories. Aim to create a budget that allows you to live within your means while setting aside money for emergencies and future goals.

Building an emergency fund is another critical step. An emergency fund provides a financial safety net in case of unexpected expenses, such as medical emergencies, car repairs, or job loss. Aim to save at least three to six months' worth of living expenses in a readily accessible account. This fund can provide peace of mind and financial stability during challenging times.

Investing in insurance is also an important aspect of financial planning.

Health insurance, life insurance, and property insurance can protect you and your assets from significant financial loss. Evaluate your current insurance policies and consider additional coverage if necessary.

Retirement planning is another key component. Ensure that you are contributing to retirement accounts, such as a 401(k) or IRA, and take advantage of employer matching contributions if available. Consider consulting with a financial advisor to develop a retirement plan that aligns with your goals and ensures financial security in the long term.

If you have joint accounts or shared assets with the narcissist, it is crucial to take steps to protect your interests. Close joint accounts and open individual accounts in your name. If closing the account is not possible, consider freezing the account to prevent further transactions without mutual consent. Notify financial institutions of the separation and request that any changes to the account require both parties' approval.

It is also wise to obtain a credit report to check for any unauthorized activity. Narcissists may open credit accounts in your name or accrue debt without your knowledge. Regularly monitoring your credit report can help identify and address any fraudulent activity promptly. If you find any discrepancies, report them to the credit bureaus and request that a fraud alert be placed on your credit file.

Establishing financial independence is crucial. This might involve opening a new bank account, applying for a credit card in your name, and ensuring your income is deposited into your personal account.

Building your credit history is essential, especially if the narcissist has damaged your credit score. Start by paying bills on time, reducing debt, and using credit responsibly.

Steps to Take if the Narcissist Controls Finances

If the narcissist has been controlling the finances, taking back control can be challenging but essential for your financial well-being. Here are steps to take if you find yourself in this situation.

First, gather as much financial information as possible. This includes account statements, tax returns, pay stubs, bills, and any other financial documents. Having a comprehensive understanding of the financial landscape is crucial for taking informed steps.

Seek the assistance of a financial advisor or accountant. A professional can help you understand your financial situation, create a budget, and develop a plan to regain control. They can also provide guidance on managing debt and rebuilding credit. Financial advisors can offer a neutral perspective and expert advice, which is invaluable in navigating complex financial issues.

If the narcissist has restricted your access to financial resources, consider seeking temporary financial assistance from trusted friends or family members. This support can provide immediate relief and help you cover essential expenses while you work on securing your financial independence.

Legal intervention may be necessary if the narcissist refuses to relinquish control or if there are significant financial disputes. Consulting with an attorney who specializes in family law or financial abuse can provide you with legal options and protections. An attorney can assist in filing for spousal support, child support, or legal separation, which can help ensure financial stability.

In some cases, courts can issue orders to prevent the narcissist from depleting assets. For example, a financial restraining order can be issued to freeze certain assets and prevent their unauthorized transfer or sale. This can be particularly important if there is a risk that the narcissist will dissipate assets out of spite or to prevent you from receiving a fair share.

Opening a new bank account in your name is a critical step. Ensure that this account is with a different bank from any joint accounts to prevent the narcissist from accessing it. Redirect your income and any direct deposits to this new account. Change your banking passwords and consider using a secure password manager to enhance security.

If the narcissist controls shared bills or credit accounts, it is important to address these as soon as possible. Contact creditors and utility companies to inform them of the separation and request that accounts be transferred to your name or closed. If you are unable to pay the bills immediately, explain your situation and ask for a payment plan or temporary hold on the account.

Rebuilding your credit is essential if it has been damaged by the narcissist's actions. Start by paying off any outstanding debts and ensuring that bills are paid on time. Consider applying for a secured credit card, which requires a cash deposit and can help rebuild your credit score over time. Regularly monitor your credit report to track your progress and identify any issues that need to be addressed.

Another crucial step is to educate yourself about personal finance. Knowledge is power, and understanding financial concepts such as budgeting, saving, investing, and credit management can empower you to make informed decisions and protect your assets. There are numerous resources available, including books, online courses, and financial workshops, that can provide valuable insights and skills.

Seeking support from a financial abuse support group can also be beneficial. These groups offer a safe space to share experiences, gain support, and learn from others who have faced similar challenges. Connecting with others who understand your situation can provide emotional support and practical advice.

If the narcissist continues to interfere with your finances, document all interactions and attempts to control or manipulate financial matters. Keep detailed records of any financial abuse, including dates, times, and specific actions taken by the narcissist. This documentation can be invaluable if legal action becomes necessary.

Finally, prioritize self-care and mental health. Financial abuse can be extremely stressful and emotionally draining. Ensuring that you take care of your physical and mental well-being is crucial. This might involve seeking therapy, engaging in stress-relief activities, and building a supportive network of friends and family.

Protecting your assets involves proactive financial planning and taking decisive steps to regain control if the narcissist controls the finances. By securing financial records, creating a budget, building an emergency fund, and seeking professional assistance, you can establish financial independence and stability. Taking legal action, opening new accounts, and educating yourself about personal finance are essential steps in safeguarding your assets and rebuilding your financial life. Prioritizing self-care and seeking support can help you navigate this challenging journey and emerge stronger and more resilient.

Custody and Co-Parenting Issues

Navigating custody arrangements and co-parenting with a narcissist can be incredibly challenging. Narcissists often use their children as tools for manipulation and control, complicating custody negotiations and creating a toxic environment for co-parenting. This section will explore strategies for navigating custody arrangements with a narcissist and protecting children from emotional harm.

Navigating Custody Arrangements with a Narcissist

When dealing with custody arrangements, it is crucial to prioritize the best interests of the children. Courts typically consider factors such as the children's safety, stability, and well-being when making custody decisions. Unfortunately, narcissists can be highly manipulative, presenting a facade of concern and competence while hiding their true behaviors. Therefore, it is essential to gather comprehensive evidence of the narcissist's behavior and its impact on the children.

Documentation is key. Keep detailed records of interactions with the narcissist, including text messages, emails, and instances of abusive or manipulative behavior. Note any concerning behavior towards the children, such as neglect, emotional abuse, or attempts to turn the children against you. This evidence can be critical in court to demonstrate the narcissist's harmful behavior and advocate for custody arrangements that protect the children.

Engaging a skilled family law attorney is crucial. An experienced attorney can help navigate the legal complexities of custody disputes, present evidence effectively, and advocate for your children's best interests. They can also help counter the narcissist's manipulative tactics, ensuring that the court sees through any false presentations.

If possible, aim for a custody arrangement that minimizes direct interaction with the narcissist. Parallel parenting, where each parent has minimal direct contact and communicates primarily through written means like email or a co-parenting app, can reduce conflict and provide a more stable environment for the children. Clear and specific custody agreements that outline detailed schedules, decision-making responsibilities, and communication protocols can help prevent the narcissist from exploiting any ambiguities.

It is also essential to establish firm boundaries and stick to them. Narcissists thrive on control and chaos, often trying to push boundaries and create confusion. By adhering strictly to the custody agreement and not deviating from the established schedule or rules, you can reduce opportunities for manipulation and maintain a more predictable environment for the children.

Seeking the assistance of a parenting coordinator or mediator can be beneficial. These professionals can facilitate communication, help resolve conflicts, and ensure that the custody agreement is followed. They can also provide a neutral perspective and keep the focus on the children's well-being, rather than getting caught up in the narcissist's manipulative tactics.

Another important aspect is to be prepared for court appearances. Narcissists can be charming and convincing in court, often portraying themselves as the more competent and loving parent. Having a clear, fact-based presentation supported by evidence can counteract their manipulative narrative. Witnesses such as teachers, therapists, or other professionals who have observed the narcissist's behavior can also provide valuable testimony.

Protecting Children from Emotional Harm

Protecting children from emotional harm is paramount when co-parenting with a narcissist. Narcissists often use children as pawns in their power games, which can have significant emotional and psychological impacts. Implementing strategies to safeguard your children's well-being is essential.

First, create a safe and supportive environment in your home. Ensure that your children feel loved, valued, and understood. Open communication is vital; encourage your children to express their feelings and concerns without fear of judgment. Providing a stable, nurturing environment can help counteract the emotional turmoil they may experience with the narcissist.

Teach your children healthy boundaries. Explain the importance of personal boundaries and help them understand that it is okay to say no and to express their needs. Empowering your children to set and maintain boundaries can reduce their vulnerability to the narcissist's manipulative behavior. Role-playing scenarios can help them practice how to assertively communicate their boundaries.

It is also important to monitor your children's emotional and psychological health. Watch for signs of distress, such as changes in behavior, mood swings, anxiety, or depression. Seeking the assistance of a child psychologist or therapist can provide your children with a safe space to process their emotions and develop coping strategies. Professional support can also offer you guidance on how to address any emotional issues your children may face.

Maintaining a sense of routine and consistency is crucial for children dealing with the instability of a narcissistic parent. Establishing regular routines for meals, homework, and bedtime can provide a sense of security and predictability. Consistency in rules and expectations can also help children feel more secure and understand that there are stable structures in their lives.

Limiting the narcissist's ability to manipulate or alienate the children is another critical aspect. Parental alienation, where one parent attempts to turn the children against the other parent, is a common tactic used by narcissists. Counteracting this requires maintaining a positive relationship with your children and not engaging in negative talk about the narcissist. Focus on reinforcing your bond with your children through quality time, positive reinforcement, and supportive communication.

If you suspect that the narcissist is attempting to alienate the children or manipulate them emotionally, document these instances meticulously. This documentation can be crucial in legal proceedings to demonstrate the narcissist's harmful behavior and advocate for custody arrangements that protect the children's well-being.

Another strategy is to create a "safe word" system with your children. This can be a word or phrase that your children can use to indicate that they are feeling unsafe or uncomfortable. Having a plan in place for how to respond when the safe word is used can provide your children with a sense of security and ensure that they know they can reach out to you for help.

Educational support is also important. Informing teachers, school counselors, and other relevant personnel about the situation can help them provide additional support and monitor your children's well-being. They can alert you to any changes in behavior or signs of distress that may arise in the school setting.

Additionally, fostering resilience in your children is key. Resilience involves the ability to cope with and recover from adversity. Encourage your children to engage in activities that build their confidence and self-esteem, such as sports, hobbies, or creative pursuits. Teaching problem-solving skills and promoting a growth mindset can also help them navigate challenges more effectively.

It is crucial to take care of your own mental and emotional health as well. Being a stable and resilient parent provides a model for your children and enables you to support them more effectively. Seeking therapy, engaging in self-care practices, and building a support network can help you manage the stress and emotional toll of co-parenting with a narcissist.

In some cases, supervised visitation or limited custody may be necessary to protect the children from emotional harm.

If the narcissist's behavior poses a significant risk to the children's well-being, advocating for supervised visits or requesting that custody arrangements be adjusted can provide an additional layer of protection. Courts can order supervised visitation to ensure that interactions between the narcissist and the children are monitored by a third party.

Navigating custody arrangements and co-parenting with a narcissist requires careful planning, firm boundaries, and a focus on the children's best interests. By documenting the narcissist's behavior, seeking legal support, and establishing clear custody agreements, you can protect your children from manipulation and emotional harm. Creating a supportive, stable environment, teaching healthy boundaries, and monitoring their emotional health are crucial steps in safeguarding their well-being. Through resilience-building activities and professional support, both you and your children can navigate the challenges of co-parenting with a narcissist and emerge stronger and more resilient.

"You don't attract narcissists because something is wrong with you. You attract narcissists because so much is right with you."

Rebuilding Self-Esteem

Rebuilding self-esteem after a relationship with a narcissist is a critical step in the healing journey. Narcissistic abuse often leaves deep emotional scars, eroding confidence and self-worth. Recovering from this experience requires a deliberate and compassionate approach to regaining confidence and fostering self-love. This section will outline steps to regain confidence and self-worth, as well as activities and practices to foster self-love.

Steps to Regain Confidence and Self-Worth

The first step in rebuilding self-esteem is to acknowledge and understand the impact of the abuse. Recognize that narcissistic abuse is a systematic effort to undermine your sense of self. By understanding this, you can begin to separate the abuser's manipulations from your true identity. It's essential to remind yourself that the negative messages you received were not a reflection of your worth but a tactic of control.

Engaging in self-reflection is vital. Take time to identify the specific ways in which the abuse has affected your self-esteem. Reflect on moments when you felt diminished, criticized, or devalued, and recognize the patterns of behavior used by the narcissist to manipulate your sense of self. This awareness is the first step towards healing and reclaiming your self-worth.

Surrounding yourself with supportive people is crucial. Seek out friends, family members, and support groups who can provide encouragement, validation, and understanding. Positive relationships can help counteract the negative messages from the narcissist and provide a network of support as you rebuild your self-esteem. Support groups, particularly those for survivors of narcissistic abuse, can offer a sense of community and shared experience that is invaluable in the healing process.

Professional therapy can also be instrumental in regaining confidence and self-worth. A therapist experienced in dealing with trauma and abuse can provide a safe space to explore your feelings, address the impact of the abuse, and develop strategies for rebuilding your self-esteem. Cognitive-behavioral therapy (CBT), in particular, can help challenge and reframe negative thought patterns, replacing them with more positive and empowering beliefs about yourself.

Setting small, achievable goals is another effective strategy. Accomplishing these goals can provide a sense of competence and boost your confidence. Start with manageable tasks that you can complete successfully, gradually increasing the complexity as your confidence grows. Celebrating these achievements, no matter how small, reinforces your ability to succeed and builds a foundation of self-efficacy.

Practicing assertiveness can also help rebuild self-esteem. Learning to express your needs, set boundaries, and stand up for yourself is empowering. Assertiveness training or workshops can provide practical skills and techniques for communicating more confidently and effectively.

As you become more comfortable asserting yourself, you will likely notice a corresponding increase in your self-esteem.

Journaling is a powerful tool for self-reflection and healing. Writing about your experiences, feelings, and progress can help you process emotions and gain insights into your journey. Journaling can also serve as a record of your growth, providing tangible evidence of your progress and resilience. Use your journal to document moments of self-doubt and counter them with positive affirmations and reflections on your strengths and achievements.

Challenging negative self-talk is essential in rebuilding self-esteem. Pay attention to the inner dialogue that occurs when you feel insecure or self-critical. Actively challenge these negative thoughts by questioning their validity and replacing them with positive, affirming statements. For example, if you catch yourself thinking, "I'm not good enough," counter this with, "I am capable and deserving of success and happiness." Over time, this practice can help shift your mindset from self-doubt to self-assurance.

Engaging in self-care activities is crucial for healing and boosting self-worth. Self-care involves taking deliberate actions to nurture your physical, emotional, and mental well-being. This might include regular exercise, healthy eating, sufficient sleep, and relaxation practices. Prioritizing self-care sends a powerful message to yourself that you are worthy of care and attention.

Activities and Practices to Foster Self-Love

Fostering self-love is a continuous process that involves embracing your worth, treating yourself with kindness, and engaging in activities that nurture your soul. Here are some practical activities and practices to help cultivate self-love.

One effective practice is daily affirmations. Affirmations are positive statements that you repeat to yourself to reinforce self-love and confidence. Examples include "I am worthy of love and respect," "I am enough just as I am," and "I deserve happiness and success." Repeating these affirmations regularly, especially in front of a mirror, can help internalize these positive messages and counteract negative self-perceptions.

Engaging in hobbies and activities that bring you joy is another way to foster self-love. Whether it's painting, dancing, gardening, or playing an instrument, immersing yourself in activities you love can boost your mood and reinforce your sense of self-worth. These activities provide a sense of accomplishment and allow you to express yourself creatively, contributing to a more positive self-image.

Mindfulness and meditation practices can also enhance self-love. Mindfulness involves paying attention to the present moment without judgment, allowing you to become more aware of your thoughts and feelings. Meditation practices, such as loving-kindness meditation, focus on cultivating compassion and love towards yourself and others. These practices can help you develop a more accepting and compassionate relationship with yourself.

Gratitude journaling is another powerful tool for fostering self-love. Each day, write down things you are grateful for, focusing on positive aspects of yourself and your life. This practice helps shift your focus from negative to positive, fostering a sense of appreciation and love for yourself and your achievements.

Spending time in nature can also be incredibly healing. Nature has a calming effect on the mind and body, providing a space for reflection and relaxation. Whether it's a walk in the park, hiking in the mountains, or simply sitting by a lake, immersing yourself in nature can help you reconnect with yourself and foster a sense of peace and self-love.

Practicing forgiveness, both towards yourself and others, is essential for healing and self-love. Holding onto past mistakes or grievances can hinder your ability to move forward and love yourself fully. Recognize that everyone makes mistakes and that these do not define your worth. Practice self-compassion by forgiving yourself for past errors and allowing yourself to learn and grow from them.

Engaging in acts of kindness, both towards yourself and others, can also foster self-love. Treat yourself with the same kindness and compassion you would offer a friend. This might include taking time to relax, indulging in a favorite treat, or giving yourself a break when needed. Extending kindness to others, through volunteer work or simple acts of generosity, can also enhance your sense of purpose and self-worth.

Seeking out positive and inspiring influences is crucial.

Surround yourself with people who uplift and support you, and seek out books, podcasts, and other media that promote self-love and personal growth. These influences can provide motivation, encouragement, and new perspectives that support your journey towards self-love.

Engaging in physical activities that you enjoy is another way to boost self-esteem and foster self-love. Exercise releases endorphins, which improve mood and overall well-being. Choose activities that you find enjoyable, whether it's yoga, swimming, cycling, or dancing. The goal is to move your body in a way that feels good and reinforces a positive connection with yourself.

Participating in creative self-expression can also be therapeutic and empowering. Activities such as painting, writing, music, or crafting allow you to express your emotions and experiences in a tangible form. Creative expression can be a powerful outlet for processing feelings and reinforcing your sense of identity and worth.

Lastly, set aside time for self-reflection and personal growth. This might involve reading self-help books, attending workshops, or engaging in therapy. Personal growth activities can help you understand yourself better, identify areas for improvement, and set goals for your future. Committing to your personal development reinforces your belief in your potential and worth.

Rebuilding self-esteem and fostering self-love after a relationship with a narcissist involves a multifaceted approach.

By acknowledging the impact of the abuse, seeking support, and engaging in deliberate practices to nurture your self-worth, you can regain confidence and develop a healthier relationship with yourself. Activities such as daily affirmations, hobbies, mindfulness, gratitude journaling, and creative expression can enhance self-love and contribute to your healing journey. Through consistent effort and self-compassion, you can rebuild your self-esteem and move forward with resilience and a renewed sense of self-worth.

Creating a New Life

After breaking free from a relationship with a narcissist, creating a new life becomes an essential part of the healing journey. This process involves setting goals, planning for the future, and rediscovering passions and interests that may have been suppressed or neglected. By taking these steps, individuals can reclaim their sense of self and build a fulfilling and joyful life. This section will explore how to set meaningful goals, plan for the future, and rediscover passions and interests.

Setting Goals and Planning for the Future

Setting goals is a powerful way to regain control and direction in your life. Goals provide a sense of purpose and motivation, helping you to focus on what is truly important to you. Start by reflecting on what you want to achieve in various areas of your life, such as career, education, relationships, health, and personal growth. It is essential to set both short-term and long-term goals, as this allows you to make steady progress while keeping an eye on your broader aspirations.

Begin with setting SMART goals—Specific, Measurable, Achievable, Relevant, and Time-bound. Specific goals are clear and well-defined, leaving no room for ambiguity. Measurable goals include criteria to track progress and determine when they are achieved. Achievable goals are realistic and attainable, considering your current resources and constraints. Relevant goals align with your values and long-term objectives. Time-bound goals have a set deadline, providing a sense of urgency and a timeline for completion.

For example, if you aim to advance in your career, a SMART goal might be: "Complete a certification course in my field within six months to enhance my qualifications and increase my chances of promotion." This goal is specific (complete a certification course), measurable (course completion and obtaining certification), achievable (realistic time frame and resources), relevant (aligned with career advancement), and time-bound (within six months).

Once you have set your goals, create a detailed action plan to achieve them. Break down each goal into smaller, manageable tasks and outline the steps needed to accomplish each task. Establish a timeline for completing these tasks, and regularly review your progress to stay on track. Adjust your action plan as necessary to accommodate any changes or challenges that arise.

Visualization techniques can also be helpful in achieving your goals. Visualizing your success and imagining the steps you will take to get there can enhance motivation and reinforce your commitment to your goals. Spend a few minutes each day visualizing yourself achieving your goals, experiencing the associated emotions and benefits.

This practice can help keep you focused and inspired.

It is also important to celebrate your achievements along the way. Acknowledge and reward yourself for the progress you make, no matter how small. Celebrating milestones reinforces your sense of accomplishment and encourages continued effort towards your goals.

Financial planning is another crucial aspect of creating a new life. Assess your current financial situation, including income, expenses, debts, and savings. Create a budget that aligns with your financial goals and priorities. Focus on reducing debt, building an emergency fund, and saving for future needs and aspirations. Consider consulting with a financial advisor to develop a comprehensive financial plan that supports your goals and provides long-term stability.

Building a support network is essential for achieving your goals and planning for the future. Surround yourself with positive, supportive individuals who encourage and motivate you. This might include friends, family, mentors, or support groups. Sharing your goals and progress with your support network can provide accountability and additional encouragement.

Rediscovering Passions and Interests

Rediscovering passions and interests is a vital part of creating a new life. Narcissistic relationships often suppress or devalue personal passions and interests, making it essential to reconnect with what brings you joy and fulfillment. Exploring new activities and rekindling old hobbies can enhance your sense of identity and enrich your life.

Start by reflecting on activities that you once enjoyed but may have abandoned during your relationship with the narcissist. Think about hobbies, creative pursuits, sports, or interests that brought you happiness and satisfaction. Make a list of these activities and consider how you can reintegrate them into your life.

Experiment with new activities to discover what excites and inspires you. Attend workshops, join clubs, or take classes in areas that interest you. Trying new things can open up new avenues of enjoyment and help you find passions you may not have previously considered. Be open to exploring a variety of interests, and give yourself permission to pursue what genuinely resonates with you.

Engaging in creative activities can be particularly therapeutic and fulfilling. Whether it's painting, writing, music, dance, or crafting, creative expression allows you to process emotions, explore your inner world, and express yourself authentically. Creativity can provide a sense of accomplishment and help rebuild self-esteem by showcasing your talents and abilities.

Physical activities are another great way to rediscover passions and improve overall well-being. Exercise not only benefits physical health but also boosts mood and reduces stress. Find physical activities that you enjoy, whether it's hiking, yoga, swimming, or team sports. Participating in regular physical activity can enhance your energy levels and provide a sense of achievement.

Traveling can also be an enriching way to rediscover passions and interests.

Exploring new places, cultures, and experiences can reignite a sense of wonder and curiosity. Whether it's a short weekend getaway or an extended trip, travel can offer a fresh perspective and inspire new interests and passions.

Volunteering is another meaningful way to reconnect with your passions. Helping others and contributing to a cause you care about can provide a sense of purpose and fulfillment. Volunteering allows you to connect with like-minded individuals, build new skills, and make a positive impact in your community.

Reading is a simple yet powerful way to explore new interests and deepen your knowledge. Whether it's fiction, non-fiction, or self-help books, reading can inspire new ideas and provide a sense of connection to a broader world. Joining a book club can also offer opportunities for social interaction and discussion.

Mindfulness and meditation practices can support the process of rediscovering passions by helping you connect with your inner self. Mindfulness involves being present and fully engaged in the moment, allowing you to notice and appreciate what brings you joy. Meditation can provide clarity and insight into your true desires and interests, guiding you towards activities that align with your authentic self.

Building a vision board can be a fun and inspiring way to explore your passions and set intentions for the future. A vision board is a visual representation of your goals, dreams, and aspirations. Collect images, quotes, and symbols that resonate with your passions and arrange them on a board.

Display your vision board where you can see it regularly, and let it serve as a source of inspiration and motivation.

Journaling can also support the process of rediscovering passions and interests. Use your journal to explore your thoughts, feelings, and experiences related to various activities and interests. Reflect on what activities make you feel energized and fulfilled, and consider how you can incorporate more of these experiences into your life. Journaling can help you gain clarity and insight into what truly matters to you.

Seeking out role models and mentors can provide guidance and inspiration as you rediscover your passions. Look for individuals who embody qualities and interests you admire, and learn from their experiences and insights. Mentors can offer valuable advice, support, and encouragement as you pursue your passions and goals.

Creating a new life after breaking free from a narcissist involves setting meaningful goals, planning for the future, and rediscovering passions and interests. By setting SMART goals, developing a detailed action plan, and building a support network, you can regain control and direction in your life. Rediscovering activities that bring you joy and exploring new interests can enhance your sense of identity and fulfillment. Through reflection, experimentation, and creative expression, you can build a fulfilling and joyful life that reflects your true self and aspirations.

Maintaining Independence

Maintaining independence after breaking free from a narcissistic relationship is a critical aspect of healing and personal growth. Independence involves not only physical and financial self-sufficiency but also emotional and psychological resilience. This section will explore strategies for staying independent and resilient and provide guidance on avoiding future toxic relationships.

Strategies for Staying Independent and Resilient

Achieving and maintaining independence requires a multifaceted approach that encompasses financial stability, emotional strength, and social support. Here are some specific strategies to help you stay independent and resilient:

1. Financial Independence:

Financial independence is foundational to maintaining overall independence. Begin by creating a comprehensive budget that outlines your income, expenses, and savings goals. Track your spending and adjust your budget as necessary to ensure you are living within your means. For instance, using budgeting apps like Mint or YNAB (You Need A Budget) can help you manage your finances effectively.

Building an emergency fund is another crucial step. Aim to save at least three to six months' worth of living expenses in a separate, easily accessible account. This fund provides a financial safety net in case of unexpected expenses or job loss, offering peace of mind and stability.

Investing in your career development can also enhance financial independence. Consider pursuing additional education, certifications, or training that can improve your skills and increase your earning potential. Networking with professionals in your field and seeking mentorship opportunities can open doors to career advancement and new opportunities.

Managing debt is another important aspect. Prioritize paying off high-interest debt first, such as credit card balances, and consider consolidating loans to lower interest rates. Developing a debt repayment plan can help you regain control over your finances and reduce financial stress.

2. Emotional Independence:

Emotional independence involves developing a strong sense of self and the ability to manage your emotions effectively. One strategy is to practice self-reflection and mindfulness. Regularly set aside time to reflect on your thoughts, feelings, and behaviors. Journaling can be a helpful tool for this practice, allowing you to process emotions and gain insights into your experiences.

Mindfulness practices, such as meditation and deep breathing exercises, can help you stay grounded and present. Apps like Headspace and Calm offer guided meditations that can support your mindfulness practice. By cultivating mindfulness, you can become more aware of your emotional responses and develop healthier coping mechanisms.

Building a strong support network is also essential for emotional independence. Surround yourself with positive, supportive individuals who respect your boundaries and encourage your growth. Regularly connecting with friends and family can provide emotional support and a sense of belonging.

Therapy can play a significant role in developing emotional independence. A therapist can help you explore your emotions, address past traumas, and develop strategies for managing stress and building resilience. Cognitive-behavioral therapy (CBT) is particularly effective for identifying and changing negative thought patterns and behaviors.

3. Setting Boundaries:

Establishing and maintaining healthy boundaries is critical for protecting your independence. Boundaries define what behaviors are acceptable and unacceptable in your relationships. Start by identifying your personal limits and values. Reflect on past experiences where your boundaries were crossed and consider what changes are necessary to prevent this in the future.

Communicate your boundaries clearly and assertively. Use "I" statements to express your needs and expectations. For example, "I need time to myself after work to relax and recharge" or "I expect mutual respect in our conversations." Being clear and direct helps others understand your boundaries and reduces the likelihood of misunderstandings.

Enforce your boundaries consistently. If someone crosses a boundary, address the issue immediately and reiterate your expectations. For instance, if a friend continually calls late at night despite being asked not to, calmly remind them of your boundary and explain why it is important. Consistency reinforces the seriousness of your boundaries and encourages others to respect them.

4. Developing Self-Reliance:

Self-reliance involves trusting your abilities and making decisions independently. One way to develop self-reliance is by setting and achieving personal goals. Start with small, manageable goals that build your confidence and gradually increase the complexity of your objectives. Celebrating your achievements, no matter how small, reinforces your ability to succeed on your own.

Learning new skills can also enhance self-reliance. Consider taking classes or workshops in areas that interest you, such as cooking, home repair, or financial management. Developing practical skills not only boosts your confidence but also reduces your dependence on others for help.

Making decisions independently is another crucial aspect of self-reliance. Practice making choices based on your values and priorities, rather than seeking approval or validation from others. Start with small decisions, such as what to eat or wear, and gradually work up to more significant choices. Reflecting on the outcomes of your decisions can help you learn and grow.

5. Building Resilience:

Resilience is the ability to bounce back from adversity and adapt to challenges. Developing a growth mindset is one strategy for building resilience. A growth mindset involves viewing challenges as opportunities for learning and growth, rather than as insurmountable obstacles. Embrace setbacks as part of the learning process and use them to develop new strategies and skills.

Practicing self-compassion is also important for resilience. Treat yourself with kindness and understanding, especially during difficult times. Acknowledge your efforts and progress, and avoid harsh self-criticism. Self-compassion fosters a positive self-image and encourages perseverance.

Engaging in regular physical activity can enhance resilience by improving your physical and mental well-being. Exercise releases endorphins, which boost mood and reduce stress. Activities like yoga, running, or even daily walks can help you stay physically and mentally strong.

6. Avoiding Future Toxic Relationships:

Avoiding future toxic relationships requires awareness, discernment, and proactive strategies. Start by reflecting on past relationships and identifying patterns of toxic behavior. Recognize red flags, such as excessive control, manipulation, or lack of respect for your boundaries. Understanding these patterns can help you spot potential issues early in new relationships.

Take time to get to know someone before committing to a deeper relationship.

Rushing into a relationship can lead to overlooking warning signs. Prioritize building a foundation of trust and respect, and observe how the person treats others, especially in stressful or challenging situations.

Trust your instincts. If something feels off or makes you uncomfortable, take it seriously. Your intuition can be a valuable guide in recognizing unhealthy dynamics. Don't ignore feelings of unease or dismiss them as irrational.

Establish and maintain healthy boundaries from the beginning. Clearly communicate your needs and expectations, and observe how the other person responds. A respectful partner will honor your boundaries and support your independence.

Seek relationships with individuals who share your values and goals. Compatibility in core values, such as honesty, respect, and mutual support, is essential for a healthy relationship. Ensure that your partner's actions align with their words, and look for consistency in their behavior over time.

Prioritize your well-being and personal growth. A healthy relationship should enhance your life, not detract from it. Focus on your goals, interests, and self-care, and avoid losing yourself in the relationship. Maintaining your independence and sense of self is crucial for avoiding toxic dynamics.

Maintaining independence and resilience after leaving a narcissistic relationship involves a combination of financial stability, emotional strength, and healthy boundaries.

By implementing strategies such as budgeting, building an emergency fund, practicing mindfulness, and setting clear boundaries, you can safeguard your independence. Developing self-reliance through goal-setting and skill-building, building resilience with a growth mindset and self-compassion, and avoiding future toxic relationships by recognizing red flags and trusting your instincts are essential steps. Through consistent effort and self-awareness, you can create a fulfilling, independent life free from toxic influences.

"A narcissist doesn't break your heart; they break your spirit. That's why it takes so long to heal."

Conclusion

Final Encouragement

As you embark on the journey of healing and rebuilding your life after escaping a narcissistic relationship, it is essential to reinforce the importance of self-care and self-respect. These elements are the foundation upon which you will build a healthier, happier future. Remember, you have already taken the most significant step by choosing to leave a toxic environment. Now, it is time to focus on nurturing yourself and celebrating your resilience.

Self-care is not just a series of activities; it is a mindset that prioritizes your well-being. It involves recognizing your needs and taking deliberate actions to meet them. This might include physical activities like regular exercise, nutritious eating, and sufficient sleep. Equally important are emotional and psychological practices such as mindfulness, meditation, and seeking therapy. Self-care means setting boundaries to protect your time and energy and saying no to demands that do not serve your well-being. It is about treating yourself with the same kindness and compassion you would offer a loved one.

Self-respect is equally crucial. It is the recognition of your inherent worth and the unwavering belief that you deserve to be treated with dignity and respect. After enduring the demeaning behavior of a narcissist, rebuilding self-respect can be challenging but immensely rewarding. Start by affirming your value and worth daily. Surround yourself with people who uplift and respect you, and distance yourself from those who do not. Pursue goals and activities that align with your values and bring you joy.

Remember, self-respect is the foundation of all healthy relationships—when you respect yourself, you set the standard for how others should treat you.

Inspirational Stories of Survivors

To inspire and encourage you on your journey, here are some stories of survivors who have successfully left narcissistic relationships and rebuilt their lives.

Sarah's Story

Sarah was in a ten-year marriage with a narcissist who systematically eroded her self-esteem and isolated her from friends and family. Despite the challenges, Sarah found the courage to leave. She sought therapy, which helped her understand the dynamics of abuse and begin the healing process. Sarah returned to school to complete her degree in social work, a dream she had put on hold. Today, Sarah works as a counselor, helping other survivors of abuse. Her journey was not easy, but she found strength in her resilience and determination to create a better life. Sarah often says, "Leaving was the hardest thing I've ever done, but it was the best decision for my well-being. I am living proof that it's possible to heal and thrive."

John's Story

John endured a controlling and manipulative relationship with his partner for five years. The constant belittling and financial control left him feeling powerless. With the support of a close friend, John developed a plan to leave.

He moved to a new city, found a job, and started attending a support group for men who had experienced emotional abuse. Through therapy and the support of his group, John learned to set boundaries and rebuild his self-esteem. He discovered a passion for photography, which became a therapeutic outlet. John now has a successful photography business and advocates for men's mental health. He shares, "Taking back my life was a journey of rediscovery. I found my passion and, more importantly, I found myself."

Emily's Story

Emily's relationship with a narcissist left her feeling worthless and trapped. The emotional and psychological abuse took a severe toll on her mental health. With the encouragement of her therapist, Emily began to document the abuse and build a case for leaving. She reached out to a local women's shelter, which provided her with the resources and support she needed to escape. Emily enrolled in art classes, which became a source of healing and expression. She eventually held an art exhibition to raise awareness about narcissistic abuse. Emily reflects, "Art saved me. It gave me a voice when I felt silenced. I want other survivors to know that there is hope and beauty after the darkness."

Carlos's Story

Carlos was in a relationship where his partner's narcissistic behavior caused him to doubt his self-worth and abilities. After a particularly harsh episode, Carlos decided he needed to make a change. He sought support from a domestic violence hotline, which connected him with resources and a support group.

Carlos pursued his passion for cooking, eventually opening a small restaurant. The journey was tough, but Carlos's dedication and love for his craft brought him success. He now uses his platform to speak about emotional abuse and encourage others to seek help. Carlos says, "Cooking was my therapy, and it gave me a new purpose. If I can rebuild my life, so can you."

These stories are testaments to the strength and resilience of survivors. They highlight that leaving a narcissistic relationship is the beginning of a journey towards healing, self-discovery, and empowerment. Each of these individuals faced significant challenges but emerged stronger and more determined to live fulfilling lives.

As you move forward, remember that healing is a journey, not a destination. There will be ups and downs, but each step you take is a victory. Celebrate your progress, no matter how small. Seek support when you need it, and always prioritize your well-being. You have the strength within you to create the life you deserve. Embrace your journey with courage and hope, knowing that brighter days are ahead.

Books:

- Disarming the Narcissist: Surviving and Thriving with the Self-Absorbed by Wendy T. Behary
- The Covert Passive-Aggressive Narcissist: Recognizing the Traits and Finding Healing After Hidden Emotional and Psychological Abuse by Debbie Mirza

Websites:

- [Psychology Today - Narcissism] (https://www.psychologytoday.com/us/basics/narcissism)
- [The National Domestic Violence Hotline] (https://www.thehotline.org/)

Support Organizations:

- Narcissistic Abuse Support Groups: Offered through local community centers or online platforms like Facebook Groups.
- Domestic Violence Hotline: 24/7 support for individuals experiencing domestic abuse: 1-800-799-SAFE (7233)

Contact Information for Hotlines and Emergency Services:

- Emergency Services: Dial 911 (USA)
- National Suicide Prevention Lifeline: 1-800-273-TALK (8255)

Checklist for Leaving a Narcissist

Leaving a narcissistic relationship requires careful planning and preparation to ensure your safety and well-being. Use this step-by-step guide to help you through the process:

1. Assess Your Safety:
  - Evaluate potential risks and threats to your safety.
  - Secure important documents such as ID, passport, birth certificate, financial records, and any legal documents.

2. Create a Support Network:
    - Reach out to trusted friends, family members, or support groups.
    - Inform them of your situation and establish a communication plan.

3. Financial Independence:
  - Open a separate bank account if possible.
  - Save money discreetly and gather evidence of financial resources.

4. Emotional Preparation:
    - Seek counseling or therapy to process your emotions and build resilience.
  - Practice self-care and prioritize your mental health.

5. Develop an Exit Strategy:
  - Plan the timing and logistics of your departure carefully.
  - Have a safe place to go, whether it's a friend's house, a shelter, or a safe location.

6. Secure Housing:
 - Explore housing options such as temporary shelters or long-term rentals.
 - Ensure your new residence is secure and inaccessible to the narcissist.

7. Legal Considerations:
 - Consult with a lawyer to understand your rights regarding custody, divorce, and restraining orders.
 - Gather evidence of abuse or manipulation for legal purposes.

8. Protect Your Digital Presence:
 - Change passwords to accounts and devices the narcissist may have access to.
 - Consider using technology to track and document any harassment or threats.

9. Execute Your Plan Safely:
 - Choose a time when the narcissist is not present or when you can safely leave without confrontation.
 - Have a bag packed with essentials ready to go at a moment's notice.

10. Seek Continued Support:
 - Stay connected with your support network and seek ongoing support from counselors or support groups.
 - Keep a list of emergency contacts handy in case you need immediate assistance.

Remember, your safety and well-being are paramount. Trust your instincts and take steps at your own pace. You deserve to live a life free from abuse and manipulation.

Incident Documentation Template:

Date: [Date of Incident]

Time: [Time of Incident]

Location: [Where the incident occurred]

Description of Incident:
[Describe what happened in detail, including any verbal, emotional, or physical abuse. Note any threats or intimidation tactics used.]

Witnesses:
[List any witnesses present during the incident, if applicable.]

Impact on You:
[Describe how the incident made you feel emotionally, mentally, or physically. Note any injuries or damages caused.]

Actions Taken:
[Document any actions you took in response to the incident, such as contacting authorities, seeking medical attention, or reaching out to support.]

Follow-up Actions:
[Note any follow-up actions needed, such as filing a report, seeking legal advice, or documenting evidence.]

Journal Entry Template:

Date: [Date of Journal Entry]

Thoughts and Feelings:
[Reflect on your emotions and thoughts regarding your current situation. Describe any triggers or concerns.]

Events of the Day:
[Document any notable events or interactions with the narcissist. Include details of any incidents or confrontations.]

Self-Care Activities:
[Describe any self-care practices you engaged in to cope with stress or anxiety.]

Goals for Tomorrow:
[Set realistic goals for yourself for the next day, focusing on your safety and well-being.]

These templates provide a structured way to record incidents and maintain a journal of your experiences during this challenging time. Use them regularly to keep track of important details and to support your documentation efforts if needed in legal or personal contexts.

Adjust the templates as necessary to fit your specific needs and preferences.